CONTENTS

TRAINING THE HUNTING DOG

TRAINING THE HUNTING DOG

BY B. WATERS,

AUTHOR OF "MODERN TRAINING," "FETCH AND CARRY," ETC

POINTER

NEW Y.   F. REST AND STREAM PUBLISHING CO

BY FOR.   BLISHING CO

i

Hand Thrown Books

West Newbury, MA

Antiquarian Reprints

This softbound edition reproduces

"Training the Hunting Dog"

as published in 1901 in an effort to bring classic antiquarian
sporting books to a wider audience than could
possibly be reached by access only to those remaining
copies of the originally published works.
Special contents of this edition copyright 2013

CHAPTER I

GENERAL PRINCIPLES

DOG TRAINING, considered as an art, has no mysteries, no insurmountable obstacles, no short cuts to success. It is a result of the patient schooling of the dog in manner analogous to that employed in the schooling of the child, with the distinction, however, that the former is prepared with a special view to a limited servitude when used in the pursuit of game.

In the furtherance of this purpose, man, by certain methods, simply diverts the efforts of the dog to his own service.

Once that his prey is found man has great powers of destruction; but as compared to the dog he is distinctly inferior as a finder. By concerted action, man and dog can find and capture much more than either could if working independently. In his search for prey the dog's purpose is distinctly selfish, as is man's, but being much inferior he, when man so wills it, must needs take the position of servant. However, his pleasure in the pursuit is so great that, even if denied possession after the prey is captured, there is still sufficient incentive to satisfy his self-interest; therefore he generally is content to exercise his best hunting effort for the pleasure he feels, with some hopes to share in the fruits.

The dog is gregarious by nature, and prefers to hunt in packs; but the concerted action of the pack, in the effort to capture its prey, is not the manner best adapted to the requirements of the sportsman, although there are certain analogies to it inasmuch as in the pack life the dog may, in the efforts of a common purpose, recognize and defer more or less to a leader. While this characteristic to hunt in company is of value to the sportsman, the manner of its exercise to best serve his purpose must be subjected to much modification and restriction in many of its parts.

When working to the gun the dog must take a place so distinctly secondary that it is that of servant. To suppress or restrict his inclination to take the leading part so far as it is against the best interests of the gun and to school him in other special knowledge for its advantage, constitute an education called training or breaking.

The art of dog training is acquired by intelligent study and practice, as proficiency in any other art is acquired. All who have the time, talent and industry may become skillful dog trainers, as all who have these qualifications may become skillful in any other accomplishment, trade or profession. But, in the education of boys and girls and men and women, there is no educational system which compensates for ignorance and inefficiency if deeply grounded on the part of the teacher, nor for incapacity if shown on the part of the pupil. There must, on the one hand, be the ability to learn how to convey knowledge, and on the other the ability to receive it, else there can be no proper progress.

The mental capacity of the dog and the knowledge necessary to serve him throughout his life are infinitely less than those which are necessary to man.

Nevertheless his manner of acquiring knowledge is in a way similar to the manner employed by man in that respect.

Some years ago, when the ability to train a dog was so rare that it was the realm of the marvelous, it by many people was considered as a "gift," a something of capability conferred by Nature; therefore, coming to the trainer quite independent of experience. At the present day, sportsmen have no faith in the skill of him whose knowledge is held to be innate from birth.

On the other hand, any system set forth as having some inherent virtue, whereby a dog may be trained quickly and thoroughly regardless of his capacity to receive training or his trainer's capacity to give it, denotes that the advocate of such system is ignorant concerning it, or else is not over-scrupulous as to the manner of treating it.

While this work will fully set forth a description of the natural qualities of the dog, their relation to field work, and the best manner of diverting them from the dog's own purposes to those of the sportsman, success in the application of its teachings depends entirely on the trainer himself.

Some natural capability on the trainer's part with some experience to supplement it is essential before any substantial progress as a teacher is reasonably to be expected. The mere reading of a work on dog training, and some hit-or-miss attempts at applying its precepts, do not constitute an education in the art.

An accomplished dog trainer is not the product of some hours of reading with a few more hours of trouble with a dog added thereto.

He who acquires the art must acquaint himself with dog nature, with the details of practical field work as they relate to setters and pointers, and, to a reasonable degree, with the manner of imparting knowledge to a creature so much lower in the scale of intelligence than himself. He, furthermore, must specially school himself in the quality of self-restraint; for, in the attempt to govern man or dog, it is essential that the governor of others should learn to govern himself.

However good the instruction may be in itself, it in no wise compensates for the inefficiency consequent to ill temper if the latter be exhibited. In short, no treatise can do more than set forth what should be done and what should not be done.

As to the natural qualifications of a. trainer, in dog training, as in all other branches of human effort, there are men who are eminently efficient and men who are incompetent. Apart from these extremes, the average man may attain to useful, practical efficiency as a trainer. To determine whether he can train or not, it is necessary to make the attempt, for without such trial he cannot know definitely anything concerning
his ability.

However good may be any instruction in respect to conducting the dog's education for the service of the gun from the foregoing remarks it is clear that the matters of patience, industry, perseverance, good temper and talent lie with the trainer himself. Incidentally, it may be remarked respect to patience and good temper, that no one can train dogs successfully without them, or, at least, a partial equivalent in perseverance and self-control; yet while they are prime requisites, they are oftenest the least observed by the impetuous amateur.

Hurry and harshness always seriously retard the dog's education instead of advancing it. In most instances the beginner gives the dog an order, then hastily proceeds in a conversational way to tell him what it all means. Failing to accomplish his purposes in a moment, he becomes irritated, warm and inclined to use force. If the dog struggle to escape from what is so amazing and painful to him, yet from what was intended to be an instructive lesson, the act begets anger and this in turn begets violence.

The transition from the A B C's to a flogging is commonly very quick, in the first attempts. Being advised so fully on this point the beginner should exercise the greatest care in observing self control and an intelligent consideration of the dog's powers; but strange to say, the advice is at first rarely heeded. Sooner or later he must learn that punishment teaches the puppy nothing useful; that it evokes distrust and resentment; that it lessens or destroys all affection for the trainer and all interest in his purposes; and that when fear dominates, the puppy, being in a disorganized state of mind, is incapable of learning even the simplest lessons. When thus intimidated his confidence must be restored by kind treatment, and then a greater degree of patience and self-restraint is necessary than was necessary before.

If the amateur would consider the days when he himself was a pupil at school he would therefrom better grasp the disadvantages under which the puppy labors. With a better intellect, with the advantages of a language both oral and written, and with more years at school than would measure twice the age of the very age old dog, the boy in comparison makes slow progress even in the rudiments. If, instead of patient treatment, the teacher shook him by the collar, cuffed his ears or kicked him in the ribs as the true method of conveying knowledge, no sensible person would expect the boy to learn much. Indeed, corporal punishment, even as a corrective, has been almost entirely abolished in the public schools. And yet the .same patient effort on the part of the teacher in educating the boy is much the same as that to be observed in the education of the dog.

Dog training, in any of its particulars, is not a matter of set forms and arbitrary methods. Each particular pupil should be developed according to his individual characteristics, and the governing circumstances. There are hundreds of little differences of dog character and capabilities to be noted and considered, and, until the trainer can perceive, understand and take advantage of them, his attempts to teach will be more or less arbitrary and mechanical.

He may now and then have some success with an arbitrary method which happens to fit a certain dog's peculiarities, but it is merely a happening.

It requires but little thought to perceive the absurdity of applying a set method alike to the nervous, the weak, the stupid, the intelligent, the lazy, the timid, the slow, the industrious, etc. Such a course of treatment must result in many failures.

Methods should be adapted to the circumstances of each individual case, compromising as much as possible with the idiosyncrasies of the pupil, with a view to obtain the best results independently of arbitrary method.

By kindness and refraining from attempts to force

progress beyond the dog's capacity, success will result in every case where it is possible. However, nothing progressive can be expected of the mentally weak, the constitutional loafer, or the dog whose nose is functionally incapable of serving up to the requirements.

The trainer may proceed on the theory that the dog learns only from practical experience; that all the advantages of oral communication possessed by man, excepting a few of limited degree, are denied to him; that his intellect and his ability to learn readily are far inferior to those of his teacher; that he needs time in which to learn, as did his teacher before him, and that in the matter of force against force, he is practically helpless.

Let the lessons be prepared and taught with a recognition that puppy hood corresponds to infancy, and thereby afford the puppy an opportunity to learn them from his standpoint. The teacher's standpoint, if it ignores dog nature and dog intellect, may be incomprehensible to him.

The dog's education proceeds on certain lines regardless of the terms used to denote it. Thus the terms "training" and "breaking" have a common application, and, as commonly used, their significance is synonymous. Either one, however, apart from their technical significance, could be construed as having a distinct meaning. For instance, it may be considered that a dog is trained to do what is right and broken from doing what is wrong. Theoretically, the former may not presuppose any punishment at all; practically, the theory is a failure. Several writers have drawn a fine distinction between the words as they relate to training, as though therein lay the fundamental principles of the art, though it is quite independent of any juggle of words. A dog trains on without punishment if he does not need it; if he does need it, it should be given to him.

Some dogs require very little punishment; others require a great deal. If the dog needs painful correction, punish him; if he does not, do not punish him. Whatever may be the choice of terms, this is the correct procedure under either; it is all a matter of training or a matter of breaking, or a matter of both as the trainer pleases. However, at no time does a dog need punishment simply because the trainer is angry at him. It then is an emotion of the trainer entirely distinct from training.

The dog is naturally fond of company. He prefers the society of his -fellows, though he recognizes the domination of man, and has a profound affection for him. Nevertheless, his purposes when seeking prey are quite independent of man and quite selfish in their unchecked, natural play. He may love his master with a fervor unlimited, but it is no factor when he is in hot pursuit. From the untrained dog's point of view, the chase and its possibilities are strictly a matter between himself and the rabbit, in manner similar to the relation between dog and dinner. The whistle, loud commands and praise, he then alike ignores. This self-interest, displayed by the dog, is an important factor in his training. There must always be sufficient incentive of a selfish nature to induce his best effort. His trainer may have some of the same property.

There are writers who solemnly affirm that the instinct to hunt is by Nature implanted in the dog for the benefit of man, or at least for such relatively small number of men as can sally forth afield to kill birds. The nature and acts of the dog oppose this egotistical opinion on every point. The dog never enjoys himself better than when on a self-hunting outing the proceeds of his efforts he needs for food and so uses when he is permitted to do so. When on his predatory excursions he rather avoids than seeks the company of man. Moreover, if the instinct were implanted in the dog for man's benefit, no training would then be necessary. The dog's natural efforts are for his own advantage. In a domesticated state he seeks his prey in a manner similar to that in which he seeks it in his predatory excursions when wild. It is his method of obtaining a food supply, the wherewithal to satisfy the cravings of hunger. Meat is his natural food. He craves it as the ox craves grass when hungry, each eating according to its nature.

Man does not care for the grass as food for himself, and not wanting it, he does not deem it worth while to assert that the ox seeks grass instinctively for the benefit of man. He does want the dog's choicest prey, therefore it is quite an easy matter to assert that the dog chases rabbits and other game for him. Such animals as he rejects he credits to the dog's own account and commends him as a great destroyer and consumer of vermin. However, as the dog is naturally carnivorous and utilizes his prey for food, the facts seem to indicate that his seeking instincts are for his own organic preservation. The dog takes a fierce pleasure in the pursuit and capture. Over and above the obtaining of a food supply thereby he finds a savage delight in them. Thus sheep-killing dogs and wolves, when they at- tack a flock of sheep, kill far more than they need for food. Most dogs will attack a rat or rats at sight, and never cease their efforts till the last one is killed or escapes.

By a course of education, either direct or indirect, all domestic dogs are taught what animals they may kill and what ones they may not. This is not always an easy task, as any one who has been out in the country with some mature, city-bred setters and pointers on their first outing can testify. The farmer's sheep and poultry then have cause for alarm.

This instinct to pursue and kill is dog nature, and moreover it is good dog nature. Checked to proper limitations and schooled to the sportsman's purposes, it is what makes the dog a useful servant. He has the inclination, intelligence and capabilities for hunting; these the sportsman applies to the furtherance of his own pleasure.

Left to his own inclination entirely, the dog hunts for himself, but his passion for hunting is so great that he will submit to much restriction in his efforts and great loss in respect to what he captures, before he will desist. Yet too much restriction may lessen his ardor; too much punishment may suppress all effort.

So far as teaching the dog how to hunt is concerned, the trainer is in that relation hardly worth considering; but he is an all-important factor in giving the dog the necessary opportunities to learn. These being given the manner of seeking or whether he seeks at all or not lies with the dog.

The beginner generally falls into the error of attempting to train the dog before the latter knows anything about practical field work. The true method is to permit the dog to seek and find in his own manner, and then school his efforts to the use of the gun. Any efforts directed toward improving the dog's natural methods of hunting are likely to end in failure, or are likely to mar them.

If a dog is naturally deficient in speed, nose, stamina, industry, intelligence, etc., no trainer can sup-ply the qualities which Nature omitted. It is impossible to make a good dog out of a naturally poor one, though the reverse is possible.

In this connection it may be mentioned that a good pedigree is not necessarily a guarantee of a good worker. A poor dog with a fine pedigree is no better than a poor dog with no known pedigree at all. The test of field merit is the test of the individual himself. The excellence of an ancestry may be something entirely apart from any qualities possessed by the individual, or it may be possessed in a greater or less degree by him ; it all is as it may happen to be. The dog as a worker must stand or fall on his own merits.

In character, intelligence, stamina, industry, selfishness and unselfishness, etc., dogs vary quite as much as men vary, and there are no hard and fast rules for the training of either. He is the best teacher of man or dog who can best understand the capabilities of his pupil, so modifying or combining methods that they are presented in the best manner to the pupil's capacity and the circumstances of the particular case. To determine nicely all these points requires close observation and good temper. The teacher must always keep in mind the two standpoints, his own on the one hand as a teacher imparting knowledge, and on the other that of the dog whose intellect is relatively weak, whose ability to acquire ideas is relatively limited, and whose nature is such that the lessons of servitude are repugnant to him. Although comparatively slow in learning the lessons inculcated by his trainer, the dog is quick to learn how best to apply his powers for the benefit of his own needs.

The beginner who feels his way carefully along will make much better progress than he whose efforts are marked by inconsiderate haste. It is easily perceived that if the trainer does not endeavor to understand the nature and capacity of his pupil, his efforts to teach will be far from good. Let the amateur consider that the dog's education is properly a matter of weeks and months instead of a matter of a few lessons carefully given or many lessons forcefully given; that the trainer's haste does not in the least add to the dog's ability or inclination to learn, and that a puppy is an undeveloped creature which needs age for the proper development of its reasoning powers.

CHAPTER II

INSTINCT, REASON AND NATURAL DEVELOPMENT

A s TENDING to a better understanding of dog nature, consequently as tending to a better application of the ways and means of a dog's education, a brief discourse on the instincts of pointers and setters, their powers of reason in the abstract and as applied to field work, and the best manner of development from the sportsman's point of view, is essential.

To the average beginner, all dogs are simply dogs, and all dogs are alike, a natural consequence to commencing as an educator without first acquiring any correct ideas as to how dogs learn and what they learn.

Indeed, without any thought of the matter even after he commences the training it never occurs to him that the apparent stupidity of his pupils may be an index of his own inability to teach.

A man may be ever so able to instruct one of his own kind, whose mental capacity, being similar, he understands, and yet be unable to instruct a dog, whose mental capacity is so dissimilar and therefore so misunderstood. Let the trainer carefully note how the dog learns; how much his intellect can compass lesson by lesson and how much as a whole; what to teach step by step and how to do it, at the same time retaining his pupil's affection and confidence. As to instinct, nothing is more difficult to define in fact, the definition of it has never been satisfactorily given by even the greatest philosophers. Abstruse speculations concerning it have been advanced, but they are in that broad realm of speculation where the intangible reigns. No one can tell how the colt, when its age is measured only by minutes, is impelled to suckle its dam and succeeds in doing so, or how it knows enough to follow her about, or how it recognizes and obeys her voice; or how young birds know how to build a nest without ever having seen one built, or how they know that it is necessary to build them at all ; or how they have the migratory impulse and know the proper direction to take when they migrate, or how the grub knows how to spin an envelope around itself, etc. The manifestations of instinct in the animal world are innumerable. Even a brief treatment of them would require a volume of space. The trainer, after reading it all, would know nothing definite concerning them save that they existed and seemed to be independent of all experience in their exercise.

Those who care to further investigate this subject will find much of interest in respect to it in "The De- scent of Man," by Darwin; "Animal Intelligence," by Romanes; "The Senses and the Intellect," by Bain; "Animal Life and Intelligence," by Morgan; "The Principles of Psychology," by James, and in works of Spencer, Wundt, Buchner, Wasman, Hume, Wesley Mills and in those of a host of other writers, German, French and English, all of whom most interestingly present much to instruct and much more to confuse the reader.

When, however, an animal consciously performs an act as a means to an end, all the recognized authorities agree that the act then comes within the domain of reason; dogs consciously plan and execute their plans at a very early age, profit by experience and display a discriminating use of their acquired knowledge.

It is impossible to draw a definite line between instinct and reason, but the two as a whole are easily distinguishable. Thus the natural impulse of the dog to hunt rabbits or birds might be termed instinctive, while the manner in which he conducts his pursuit of them in his efforts to capture is an act of reason.

The dog's physical structure closely resembles that of man. His brain is somewhat similar in shape and material to man's and it relatively serves the same purposes. Like man, the dog gains a knowledge of the external world through the means of his senses hearing, seeing, tasting, feeling and smelling, the latter being the one most used and the most keenly developed.

The common, everyday life of the dog in and about the home of man displays in innumerable ways a keen perception of cause and effect. He learns to a nicety what privileges are permitted to him, at what time and place and of whom he may expect to receive his food, what, people are most friendly to him, what places afford the most comfortable sleeping quarters for summer or winter, what dogs of the neighborhood best romp or hunt to his liking, etc.

All his acts are founded on knowledge acquired by experience. As instincts are quite independent of experience, the distinction is apparent. All instincts are much alike as displayed, one animal with another. They may vary in the degrees of intensity, but they are the same in kind. The mother's love for her offspring, the instinct of self-preservation, etc., are manifested much alike by every individual. On the other hand, acts of reason vary greatly in their manifestations concerning the same object. For instance, out of several methods by which a purpose may be accomplished, as in the pursuit of a rabbit, some dogs adopt one method, some another, according to the governing circumstances at the time, such as the dog's knowledge of methods derived from prior experience ; his ability to discriminate as to methods ; his ability as to bodily powers that is, whether he has sufficient speed to rush and capture at once, or, being slow, whether to make a long race on the basis of endurance, etc. The same dog, indeed, not infrequently employs different methods at different times to accomplish the same purpose accordingly as experience improves his knowledge or maturity improves his intellect, or as different circumstances govern, such as whether he is working alone or as one of a pack, etc.

Instinct holds relatively as small part in the life of the dog as it does in the life of a man. Dogs inherit the instinct of self-preservation, the maternal and paternal instinct and the instinct to seek a food sup- ply, etc., but in the activities of life, in choosing means to ends, their intelligence holds full sway.

The dog's knowledge is a growth. Whether he is wild or domesticated, he has much training of mind and body to undergo before he fits into his environment to the best advantage to himself. If in a wild state, he must learn all the wiles of pursuit, of attack and defense, both as an individual and as one of a pack. In a domesticated state he intelligently fits himself to his environment by following the lines of least resistance. Cuffed for jumping on the bed, driven from the parlor with a broomstick, scolded for barking in the house or thrashed for an attempt to steal food from the table, etc., he avoids the experiences which are painful and makes the most of such privileges as are pleasant and allowed to him.

In time, as experience directs, his manner of life becomes his habit of life. He ceases to have a longing for the comforts of the parlor and forbears stealing food unless he has a safe opportunity.

The moral nature of the dog never reaches to a height which commands much confidence. He is naturally a predatory animal, and his marauding instincts, though reasonably dormant in his own home, are quickly brought into activity on outside opportunity. In the home of his master's friend, where he is for the first time, he most brazenly searches every nook and corner, disregards his home manners and does not hesitate to appropriate to his own use any food he may find. According to his point of view he is doing no wrong. Such is his nature.

In time, with more thumpings and more painful experience, he learns that the rules in force at his own home are also the rules to be observed when he is in other homes, and he governs himself accordingly. However, he easily drifts into vagabond habits if opportunity offers, such as sneaking off into the fields and woods on self-hunting trips, associating with vagabond dogs, etc., and at such times he will indulge in many freaks and fancies of which he would not be guilty if under the eye of his master.

He has a profound affection for his master, but that does not in the least signify that he loses any of his own individuality or interest in his own manner of life.

On the matter of his affection, by the way, he has been

lauded to heights, on the one hand quite as unwarranted as he has been depreciated on the other in the matter of intelligence. Dogs love their masters, it is true, but not as a rule with the loyalty and devotion so dear to sentimental writers as a theme when elaborating on the nobility which dogs possess.

The average dog, however much he may exhibit affection for his master to-day, will be quite content to take up with a new one to-morrow. A few appetizing morsels of food are sufficient to excite his interest, a few pats on the head evoke his friendship, and a few repetitions of friendly attention w r in his affection. Some dogs have a more consistent devotion than others ; some are brave and will fight for their masters as they will fight for each other ; some will run from danger, regardless of whom it may threaten, and in all this they resemble some men.

The dog, being gregarious, has a natural repugnance to loneliness. In a wild state, he lives in packs with his fellows, and observes much the same watchfulness and devotion to the common good that he does toward his home in domestication.

The wild instinct of friendly alliance is expressed in domestication. He forms an attachment for his master and the members of his master's family. He may, however, form a more friendly attachment for a horse. He concedes the domination of his master, but he concedes the same to the leader of the pack in a wild state.

The dog in domestication soon learns to consider his master's home as his own. If he prowls away from home, seeking to investigate other homes, the dogs of the latter consider that their homes are invaded, and they bark furious resentment, or perchance fight and give the intruder a sound mauling. The strange youths throw rocks at or maltreat him if they can lay hands on him. Thus he learns that his own home is the most pleasant to him. He does not know of any other home, so that accepting the best home of which he has any knowledge is not a matter deserving of any special eulogy.

Some writers have not hesitated to exalt the dog as being, in many noble characteristics, superior to man. His devotion, fidelity and unselfishness are favorite themes. Nevertheless, on analysis, all these qualities, as exhibited by the dog, are found to be far short of the ideal perfection ascribed to him. The man who first said "The more I see of men the better

I like dogs" could hardly have been serious, or, if he was serious, he knew neither men nor dogs profoundly, assuming that he had a normal mind. The dog as we find him is companionable and devoted enough. Man, nevertheless, could lose the companionship of the dog much better than the dog could that of man. In material advantages he is a gainer by his association with man.

On the question of animal intelligence, the eminent philosopher, Dr. Ludwig Buchner, in his work, Man in the Past, Present and Future," sets forth that,

"Indeed, it is sufficiently well known that the intellectual life of animals has hitherto been greatly underestimated or falsely interpreted, simply because our closet philosophers always started, not from an impartial and unprejudiced observation and appreciation of Nature, but from philosophical theories in which the true position, both of man and animals, was entirely misunderstood.

But as soon as we began to strike into a new path, it was seen that, intellectually, morally and artistically, the animal must be placed in a far higher position than was formerly supposed, and that the germs and first rudiments even of the highest intellectual faculties of man are existent and easily demonstrable in much lower regions. The pre-eminence of man over the animal is therefore rather relative than absolute that is to say, it consists in the greater perfection and more advantageous development of those characteristics which he possesses in common with animals, all the faculties of man being as it were prophetically foreshadowed in the animal world, but in man more highly developed by natural selection. On closer consideration, all the supposed specific distinctive characters between man and animals fall away, and even those attributes of humanity which are regarded as most characteristic, such as the intellectual and moral qualities, the upright gait, and free use of the hands, the human physiognomy and articulate language, social existence and religious feeling, etc., lose their value or become merely relative as soon as we have recourse to a thoroughgoing comparison founded on facts. In this, however, we must not, as is usual, confine our attention to the most highly cultivated

Europeans, but must also take into the account those types of man which approach most nearly to the animals and which have had no opportunity of raising themselves from the rude, primitive, natural state to the grade of the civilized man. In such a study as this, just as in the investigation of the animal mind, we at once arrive at the knowledge of quite different things from what the closet philosophers in their pretentious but hollow wisdom have hitherto endeavored to make us believe, and we ascertain immediately that the human being in his deepest degradation or in his rudest primitive state approaches the animal world so closely that we involuntarily ask ourselves where the true boundary line is to be drawn. Whoever wishes to form a judgment as to the true nature of man or his true position in Nature must not, as our philosophers and 'great thinkers' usually do, leave out of consideration the primeval origin and developmental history of man, and looking merely at his own little self in the delusive mirror of self-esteem, abstract therefrom a pitiable portrait of a man after the philosophical pattern. He must, on the contrary, grasp at Nature itself with both hands and draw his knowledge from the innumerable springs which flow here in the richest abundance."

Commenting further in this connection, he writes: "The second volume of his (Buchner's) 'Physiological Pictures' will also contain an essay upon the mind of animals. In this essay it will be shown by numerous well-authenticated examples and facts that the intellectual activities, faculties, feelings and tendencies of man are foreshadowed in an almost incredible degree in the animal mind. Love, fidelity, gratitude, sense of duty, religious feeling, friendship, conscientiousness and the highest self-sacrifice, pity and the sense of justice and injustice, as also pride, jealousy, hatred, malice, cunning and desire of revenge, are known to the animal, as well as reflection, prudence, the highest craft, precaution, care for the future, etc. nay, even gormandizing, which is usually ascribed to man exclusively, exerts sway also over the animal. Animals know and practice the fundamental law and arrangements of the State and of society, of slavery and caste, of domestic economy, education and sick nursing ; they make the most wonderful structures in the way of houses, caves,
nests, paths and dams ; they hold assemblies and public

deliberations and even courts of justice upon offenders; and by means of a complicated language of sounds, signs and gestures they are able to concert their mutual action in the most accurate manner. In short, the majority of mankind have no knowledge or even suspicion what sort of creature an animal is."

Darwin, in his great work, the "Descent of Man," has a paragraph in the chapter "On the Affinities and Genealogy of Man" whose import is specially to the point. He remarks: "Some naturalists, from being deeply impressed with the mental and spiritual powers of man, have divided the whole organic world into three kingdoms the human, the animal and the vegetable thus giving to man a separate kingdom. Spiritual powers cannot be compared or classed by the naturalist, but he may endeavor to show, as I have done, that the mental faculties of man and the lower animals do not differ in kind, although immensely in degree. A difference in degree, however great, does not justify us in placing man in a distinct kingdom, as will perhaps be best illustrated by comparing the mental powers of two insects, namely, or scale insect and an ant, which undoubtedly belong to the same class. The difference is here greater than, though of a somewhat different kind from, that between man and the highest mammal. The female coccus, while young, attaches itself by its proboscis to a plant, sucks the sap, but never moves again, is fertilized and lays eggs, and this is its whole history. On the other hand, to describe the habits and mental powers of the worker-ants would require, as Pierre Huber has shown, a large volume. I may, however, briefly specify a few points. Ants certainly communicate information to each other and several unite for the same work or for games of play. They recognize their fellow ants after months of absence and feel sympathy for each other. They build great edifices, keep them clean, close the doors in the evening and post sentries. They make roads as well as tunnels under rivers, and temporary bridges over them by clinging together. They collect food for the community, and when an object too large for entrance is brought to the nest they enlarge the door and afterward build it up again. They store up seeds of which they prevent the germination and which, if damp, are brought up to the surface to dry. They go out to battle in regular bands and freely sacrifice their lives for the common weal. They emigrate according to a pre-concerted plan. They capture slaves.

They move the eggs of their aphides, as well as their own eggs and cocoons, into warm parts of the nest, in order that they may be quickly hatched, and endless similar facts could be given. On the whole, the difference between the mental powers of an ant and a coccus is immense; yet no one has ever dreamed of placing these insects in distinct classes, much less in distinct kingdoms. No doubt the difference is bridged over by other insects; and this is not the case with man and the higher apes. But we have every reason to believe that the breaks in the series are simply the result of many forms having become extinct."

These extracts, given for the reader's consideration, present the convictions of men who have made this and related subjects a lifelong study, whose opportunities for acquiring information were relatively unlimited and whose mental equipment fitted peculiarly well to the exactions of their chosen field of research, all of which qualified them for the making of sound conclusions.

There is a comprehensive literature on this subject,

extremely interesting in itself. It is only incidentally related to the subject of training, yet it is worthy the attention of him who earnestly seeks a broad knowledge of it. Before making pertinent investigation on either subject, it is not difficult to believe that the dog acts wholly by instinct and that the world is flat; after unprejudiced investigation it is impossible to believe either.

Considered as a being, physically and mentally, the dog develops much after the manner of man, but with restrictions imposed by Nature and by man which force him to recognize his inferiority and dependence through life.

Superior force is a quantity in life to which all must yield. Men feel its mandates; even nations must bow to it. As between man and dog, the latter from puppyhood is taught submission and dependence. There is sufficient force at every point to repel all attempts which are obnoxious to man, his master. He recognizes this from an early age and grows into dog-hood with a full acceptance of it. The exceptional dog, which betimes has the idea that he has force enough to meet force, generally goes violently into the bourne provided for bad dogs, whence they never return. Heredity tends to the perpetuation of the dogs which are most submissive. The destruction of dogs which are of a bad or unsuitable temper weeds out the most savage, and insures the perpetuation of those which most amiably accept the place in domestication assigned to them by man.

Thus, they grow up deferential by habit, dependent from inferiority, and gregarious by nature.

The life of the dog is relatively short. At ten years he is in old age. Few dogs live so long; still fewer live much longer.

In the first year of the dog's life he goes through the same relative course of development that the boy goes through in the first dozen years of his life.

For a time the puppy is entirely helpless and dependent. Gradually strength comes, and he moves about without any exhibition of intelligence. As the brain develops, the mind begins to act, and he shows signs of ideas. Soon play engrosses his attention, and this phenomenon of his life, although by the average man considered frivolous and undesirable, is essentially useful.

It is better to let him develop in his own manner till he is a year old before the serious attempt at training is made. Give him unlimited opportunity to learn by taking him frequently into the woods and fields, and permitting him to range and seek and chase in his own manner.

The period of youth is a period of development. Nature utilizes it in the most beneficent and proper manner. It is the preparatory stage for the tasks of mature life. Therefore, until the mind and body have been developed in their powers according to Nature's laws, the puppy is not old enough to attempt his education.

Puppies play furiously with each other till they are exhausted by fatigue. After a short rest they may resume their frolics with unabated ardor. They simulate a close imitation of pursuit and escape, of cunning attack and crafty evasion, or of ambush or battle, dog against dog, seizing, wrestling and struggling in play as they do in actual fight, with the difference, however, that they use their teeth in a "make-believe" way, and do not intentionally hurt each other. At times the sham battle may develop into a real one, and then there is but little difference in the struggle save that teeth are used in earnest.

This exercise develops the dog's muscles, his power of actively using his bodily capabilities and his mental qualities, and he therefrom acquires a knowledge of his own forces and limitations. If he has no companion of his own kind, he goes through much the same fierce training with an old shoe or other object, which he tosses about, shaking and rending it, while following the instincts of his nature in the evolution as an organism, though only feeling that he is having a glorious diversion.

All these experiences are of infinite value to him by way of experimentation.

The knowledge acquired in rending, tearing, lifting, dodging, ambushing and in developing strong muscular activity, etc., is essential to him in his mature life, either in his wild or domesticated state. In a wild state it is indispensable to his existence; in a domesticated state serviceable as a means of attack and self-defense to him. His curiosity is also a factor in his development. It leads him to unlimited investigation, and thereby his nose acquires a functional power of discrimination which is specially serviceable to him.

Repress what may be wrong, such as the chasing of poultry and sheep, etc., but leave him to his uninterrupted pleasure otherwise. He learns the practical parts of life from his own experience, and by observing the doings of his fellows, but he learns only from opportunity.

Dogs are imitative. They readily learn by ob- serving the doings of older, wiser and more experienced dogs. They have a limited language by which they can convey certain ideas, and they interpret quite intelligently the significance of certain actions of each
other and of their masters.

With a purpose to give the reader some ideas on this point, as well as to evoke more serious thought in respect to it, the following from "The Descent of Man," by Darwin, is presented. Treating of language, he remarks : "This faculty has justly been considered as one of the chief distinctions between man and the lower animals. But man, as a highly competent judge, Archbishop Whately remarks, 'is not the only animal that can make use of language to express what is passing in his mind, and can understand more or less what is so expressed by another.' In Paraguay the Cebus azara, when excited, utters at least six distinct sounds, which excite in other monkeys similar emotions. The movements of the features and the gestures of monkeys are understood by us, and they partly understand ours, as Rengger and others declare. It is a most remarkable fact that the dog, since being domesticated, has learned to bark in at least four or five distinct tones. Although barking is a new art, no doubt the wild parent species of the dog expressed their feelings by cries of various kinds. With the domesticated dog, we have the bark of eagerness, as in the chase; that of anger as well as growling; the yelp or howl of despair, as when shut up ; the baying at night ; the bark of joy, as when starting on a walk with his master, and the very distinct one of demand or supplication, as when wishing for a door or window to be opened. According to Houzeau, who paid particular attention to the subject, the domestic fowl utters at least a dozen significant sounds.

"The habitual use of articulate language is, however, peculiar to man; but he uses in common with the lower animals inarticulate cries to express his meaning, aided by gestures and the movement of the muscles of the face. This specially holds good with the more simple and vivid feelings, which are but little connected with our higher intelligence. Our cries of pain, fear, surprise, anger, together with their appropriate actions, as the murmur of a mother to her beloved child, are more expressive than any words. That which distinguishes man from the lower animals is not the understanding of articulate sounds, for, as everyone knows, dogs understand many words and sentences. In this respect they are in the same stage of development as infants between the ages of ten and twelve months, who understand many, words and short sentences, but yet cannot utter a single word. It is not the mere articulation which' is our distinguishing character, for parrots and other birds possess this power. Nor is it the mere capacity of connecting definite sounds with definite ideas, for it is certain that some parrots which have been taught to speak, connect unerringly words with things and persons with events. The lower animals differ from man solely in his almost infinitely larger power of associating together the most diversified sounds and ideas, and this obviously depends on the high development of his mental powers."

In reference to this subject, besides giving his own views at greater length, he quotes from a number of authorities, who contribute valuable information, and who concur in their opinions.

But, as remarked hereinbefore, so far as the training of the dog for field work is concerned, no ideas can be communicated to him by means of speech. Such things as are useful to him in the struggles of life he learns readily, and such as are useful to his master he is taught with difficulty.

In his place in domestic life he learns the significance of what affects his own comfort or interests. He learns to interpret correctly his master's frown or smile, and learns to know by the tone of his voice whether he is pleased or displeased. His watchfulness, so much and so thoughtlessly lauded as the expression of his devotion to man, is merely the instinctive watchfulness necessary to his safety in a wild state, and is a characteristic which he would exercise quite as readily for his own kind and the preservation of his lair as he would for the benefit of man. When he barks at strange dogs or gives warning at night of the approach of strangers it should not be overlooked that he considers his own home is disturbed, though it also may be the home of his master. Much depends on the point of view.

It may be remarked further that on the one hand while the intelligence of the dog has been grossly underrated by superficial observers. it has been on the other hand quite as unreasonably exaggerated by enthusiastic admirers. The dog is not more intelligent than are many other kinds of animals, and is inferior in this respect ID some of them. He is not to be compared to man in this matter. Indeed, intelligence in the dog equal to that possessed by man would be a most grievous calamity to him. His intelligence, however, is of a high order. It is quite equal to the demands of his nature, and to his position in the scale of organic being.

29

There are writers who urge still greater claims for the dog than the claim of high intelligence. They maintain that dogs possess souls and therefore have eternal life, but that speculation is not pertinent to the best methods of training, and therefore not pertinent to this work.

His reasoning powers are quite acute on such matters as come within his immediate observation. A few of many common acts will be mentioned. Some hounds, after repeated chases of a fox over the same course, will, in some later chase, lie concealed at a point which will intercept him as the other hounds in pursuit drive him by. Greyhounds soon learn to run cunning." Setters and pointers sometimes learn to leave the trail of an old cock running down wind, circling around him till they head him off and stop his running, and pointing him then accurately. All this is reasoning by the dog over concrete subjects within his immediate observation. If an attempt were made to teach him that x represented an un- known quantity, his mind could not grasp the abstract idea, and failure would result. Primitive man displays but little more intelligence. Such as it is and so far as it goes, it is the same in kind as the intelligence displayed by the dog. In either case a vast store of knowledge pertaining to the ways and means of practical living is necessary in the struggle for existence.

As to his best development, it must be in accordance with his own nature. He must have all the liberty which can be consistently given to him, to the end that his bodily and mental powers be developed to their best limits. He must be treated kindly, so that his attachment to his master will be deep and lasting; that is to say, associating with his master and hunting with him as a companion confer one of the highest degrees of pleasure of which he has any knowledge. It should be made to him a source of constant delight. Play with his fellows, chasing butterflies and little birds, crude attempts at chasing rabbits, galloping over the fields in the wantonness of surplus energy and ecstatic spirits, and gratifying his curiosity as to the meaning of things, etc., are quite serious enough by way of occupation during the months of his puppyhood.

Many amateurs proceed on the theory that if left to himself the puppy will learn many things that are wrong, that from the beginning he must be under constant supervision, and that therefore his development must be in accord with certain finished educational standards useful to the gun. No theory could be more fallacious. The true practice, it may be reiterated, is to permit the dog to develop in his own natural manner, and then so train him that his efforts are made subservient to the purposes of the gun.

CHAPTER III

NATURAL QUALITIES AND CHARACTERISTICS

THE natural instincts of the dog and his manner of seeking prey are by the sportsman termed natural qualities. The term is used more in connection with field trial competition, to distinguish between what is natural and what is educational.

Like other members of the carnivorous family, to which he belongs, the dog is a meat eater. In securing a food supply, he naturally takes to the pursuit of other animals which are his prey. His teeth are large, strong and sharp, are set in correspondingly heavy, muscular jaws, and his digestive organs also denote that he belongs to the carnivora. He possesses extraordinary fleetness of foot, bodily activity, courage, great powers of endurance, keen and discriminating functional powers of nose and a high degree of intelligence in his sphere of .life, all of which are essential to his existence in a wild state, and in domestication are highly prized by man.

Without a high degree of intelligence, the possession of his destructive bodily powers would be of little value to him. They would be worthless if he were brainless.

Intelligence and knowledge are essential to the dog, both in respect to attack and defense. His every act denotes that he has the intelligence and capacity to acquire such knowledge as he needs. He plans craftily and executes according to his plans, or changes them to conform to varying circumstances. His acts are marked by great courage and dash when in pursuit and attack, and by great prudence and activity when in flight from danger. He possesses a certain sagacity in recognizing a superior force, and in refraining from the attack when the disadvantages are too great for probable success.

Singly, he does not hesitate to attack smaller animals than himself; larger animals he prefers to attack with the aid of his fellows that is to say, as a pack. A brief experience suffices to teach him which are the most vital parts of the animals he pursues as prey, and he inflicts injury on them accordingly.

Different dogs employ different methods of attack, according to their powers ; for instance, a large dog, battling with a woodchuck or other small animal, rushes in, catches it in the middle of the back, crushes in its spine and ribs, paralyzing and killing it quickly. Not possessing the power to kill in such a summary manner, the small dog seizes by the throat, shakes the woodchuck till it is dazed and unconscious, and holds on till he slowly kills it. If he is not strong enough to shake it, he holds it fast by the throat, thereby insuring the least possible injury to himself while inflicting the greatest possible injury on his prey, as this hold simultaneously attacks the jugular, the windpipe, many important nerves, etc. The fact that dogs employ so many different methods is alone sufficient to prove that they possess reasoning powers.

Dogs, fighting in packs, perform at their best in securing their prey. Two dogs, fighting conjointly, making common cause against an animal, are relatively far more destructive than they are fighting singly, for while one engages the enemy in front the other has a comparatively unhindered opportunity to bite and maim the rear. Several dogs in a pack therefore are exceedingly formidable when battling against other animals. They time and direct their efforts most intelligently in support and in defense of each other.

In the concerted action of all in the attack on a large animal, each may perform quite a distinct part, yet all their efforts are directed to the attainment of the same end. Some may engage the animal in a sham attack in front while others, behind, hamstring it, or tear its flanks. Turn as it may, the attack is incessantly maintained, and every vulnerable point is seized and injured till the animal weakens. At the proper juncture the pack closes in on it and then the end soon comes.

In their methods of pursuing and capturing their prey all dogs possess many traits in common. Some, however, have special qualities for one kind of pur- suit, some have them for other kinds, and these qualities peculiarly fit them for the service of man when he attempts pursuit himself.

The foxhound has the speed, stamina and nose so essential in the most successful pursuit of deer and foxes. Man is deficient in these qualities, so he appropriates the efforts of the dog to his own use. The greyhound has the dashing speed and determination which enable him to catch the swiftest hares or wolves, etc., in a short pursuit.

Setters and pointers are particularly prized by man for their natural impulse to hunt game birds, and the natural methods they employ in their efforts to capture them, for it so happens that the methods employed by the dog for himself are equally useful to man when employed in his service. As setters and pointers are naturally of an amiable and deferential nature, diverting their efforts to the purposes of the gun is not a task of great difficulty.

The contention made herein that pointing is implanted in the dog by Nature for his own benefit, and that it is but one detail of many others in the exercise of his instinctive efforts to obtain a food supply, is opposed to some exceedingly venerable teachings on this subject. That the reader may have a better understanding of the ancient speculation concerning the origin of the act of pointing, and at the same time the exalted importance of man, as determined by himself, the following excerpt is quoted from Stonehenge, whom the public, in his day and for some years afterward, accepted as an authority on this point:

In his work, "The Dogs of the British Islands" (edition of 1867), he writes: "As some difference of opinion appears to exist with regard to setters, we have determined thoroughly to satisfy ourselves as to their origin and best form, and we have called all the best authorities to our assistance. We propose to place the result of our labors before the public, and to add our own conclusions.

"There is no doubt that the sport of hawking was known and practiced by the ancient Britons, and that the Roman was totally ignorant of the science; but the invader at once came to the conclusion that the system might be improved and introduced the land spaniel, if not the water dog also, into this country.

"These dogs roused the game, and this was all that the hawker required of them in those early days; but in after years, as we shall see, dogs were required to point, or, in the language of the quaint old writer, 'Sodainely stop and fall down upon their bellies/ and having so done, when within two or three yards, 'then shall your setter stick and by no persuasion go further till yourself come in and use your pleasure.

"At first, then, without doubt, the spaniel was merely used as a springer for the hawk, which was subsequently neglected for the net; and the propensity of the dog to pause before making his dash at game was cultivated and cherished, by breeding and selection, until at last, gratified by observing the action of the net, he yielded his natural impulse of springing at all and set or lay down to permit the net to be drawn over him. After this the hawker trained his spaniel to set; then he cast off his hawk, which ascended in circles, and 'waited on' until his master roused the quarry from its concealment, when she pounced upon it like a pistol shot.

"When used either with hawks or for the net (especially in the latter case), a far heavier dog answered the purpose than what we call a 'high-ranging setter.' The net enveloped a whole covey in its meshes and few manors would allow of many coveys being taken in a day; whilst the disentangling the birds and securing them allowed time for the heavy dog to rest and regain his wind."

As further bearing on this point, he refers to it again in the same work, in the chapter on the Sussex spaniel, as follows: "About the year 1555 a Duke of Northumberland trained one 'to set birds for the net,' and soon afterward the setter was produced; either by selection or by crossing the Talbot hound and spaniel."

From the implication in the foregoing for the origin of the setter as well as the act of pointing is therein only matter of implication it was but a short step for later and more superficial writers to assert that the setter had a spaniel origin, and that the act of pointing had its source in the training of a few dogs to lie down while a net was spread over them and the covey which they had found. Could anything be more inconsequential in the explanation of a simple subject than that in 1555 an unknown Duke trained a Sussex spaniel "to set birds for the net and soon afterward the setter was produced, either by selection or by crossing the Talbot hound and the spaniel"? As to the origin of the setter, there is but one sensible conclusion that is to say, we do not know what it is. Up to the time of Col. Hutchinson there were few authors on canine subjects who wrote from their own practical experience, and fewer still who had proper discriminating powers of mind to comprehend the dog as he is, and to write of him accordingly. They accepted all the absurdities, conjectures and vagaries of the first writers as being good matter-of-fact, and did not hesitate to repeat them as being true.

By the simple process of dint of repetition, it has come to be a general belief that the pointing instinct originated as told in the net-and-dog story, or as implied by it, for it does not assert it. In fact, it admits the existence of the instinct, as shown by the remark "and the propensity of the dog to pause before making his dash at game was cultivated and cherished, by breeding and selection, until, at last, gratified by observing the action of the net, he yielded his natural impulse of springing at all," etc. That is precisely the case to-day, if we substitute the gun for the net and interpret the loosely written description according to the facts.

The dog of to-day has naturally the pause before making his dash to capture. He only forbears springing as a consequence of much training. After he has observed the success of the gun on the one hand, and after being firmly denied the pleasure of springing on the other hand, we come to the ancient and modern belief wherein he is "at last, gratified by observing the action of the net," etc. The ancient writers were, moreover, handicapped by the overweening belief in the sublimity of man and the special creation of all the lower animals for his benefit.

Considering setters and pointers from the same unprejudiced standpoint from which we would consider tigers, wild dogs, cats and rats, etc., we observe that they possess the hunting instinct and the knowledge of the best manner of hunting, to the end that they may obtain a food supply. In a wild state their existence depends on their ability to pursue and capture. The hunting instinct and the manner of its exercise were no more implanted in the nature of pointers and setters to please or profit a man with a gun than was the like instinct, etc., of their wild congeners, the wolves, dingoes, etc., implanted for the same purpose.

Setters and pointers, though their names might seem to indicate otherwise, display no essential differences in their methods of pursuit and capture, nor in their choice of prey. They delight in hunting rabbits, squirrels and other small animals, and prefer them to game birds as an object of pursuit. It is not at all a difficult matter to break a dog from hunting birds. Not infrequently the amateur accomplishes this result unintentionally and unexpectedly by punishment in his mistaken attempts to train, the result being an unfortunate condition called "blinking."

It is a task of extreme difficulty to break the dog from his passionate fondness for hunting rabbits. He for a time will disobey commands, ignore punishment and strike out independently to gratify his fondness for chasing them. On their trail he gives tongue merrily and flies along at his topmost speed, through punishing brier or muddy swamp, never feeling fatigue while the ardor of the chase is upon him.

The setter and pointer, when seeking birds, range about till they strike the trail; then they follow it carefully, silently and alertly. As the setter nears the birds and the scent gets warmer, he feathers; his eyes glisten; his jaws open tremulously; he crouches as he draws nearer, and mayhap he may drop to the ground for a moment; his nerves and muscles become tenser in anticipation of the approaching spring and dash into the concealment of the birds, and of the resultant bloody ending. The pointer exhibits the same phenomena, except the feathering.

The nose of the pointer or setter is his highest organ of sense. It has wonderful functional powers, and by experience he acquires equally wonderful powers of discrimination in its use. Each follows the trail accurately by his powers of scenting. When he has drawn near to the birds he has a new problem to solve; he must accurately determine the whereabouts of the birds in their concealment. If he cannot do so, his skill and silence in reading them avail nothing. The birds have probably discovered that an enemy is about and have sought the most convenient cover for safety. When near to them he sets, stands or points, terms which denote the same act ; he is in a position to spring to the extent of his capabilities; his eyes are set but are nevertheless keenly alert. If he is not quite sure of his distance and the location of the birds, he moves, perhaps taking a better advantage of the wind and ground, and points again.

Satisfied at length that he has made his calculations correctly, he springs from his point with wonderful agility and generally with admirable precision, succeeding frequently in catching a bird before it can get well on the wing, or before it can disentangle itself from the cover in which it was concealed.

If he has erred in his calculations or if he has not used his nose truly, he may spring from his point in a wrong direction and thereby possibly make a failure of the effort. When the birds rise the dog's eyes come into service. If he errs on the first spring he may readjust for the second, and if there are any laggards or weak birds he still may succeed in capturing one. If he captures and is permitted to dispose of the bird as he pleases, he forthwith eats it with great relish. The fox observes a similar method when he attempts to capture grouse. The cat too, exhibits analogous method in its attempt to stalk small birds, etc., trusting, however, more to the sense of sight than to the sense of smell.

Many centuries ago man observed this trait of the dog and learned that, by restraining it to limits which did not permit of the spring to capture, it could be usefully applied to his own purposes in the pursuit and capture of game birds.

Ranging, reading, pointing and the knowledge and crafty application of them which comes only from experience, the trainer cannot supply. The majority of amateurs, however, start on the mistaken theory that they must not only teach the dog how to work to the gun, but how to hunt birds.

Dogs so taught, or rather so untaught, become abjectly

perfunctory. They lose all independence of action or purpose, and look to their trainer for orders at every turn. All idea of initiative is gone from them and therewith nearly all of self-interest; consequently they are more or less listless and slothful in manner and are devoid of ardor and industry. Let the puppy range and locate the birds in his own wild way. Let him alone. What if he flushes and chases? All the better. A puppy which will not flush and chase at first is a marvel. Left to himself, he learns to locate quickly and discriminates as to the kind of cover and the nooks which the game frequents. With more experience he will modify his puppy ways; at all events, the qualities useful to man have been developed by sensible opportunity and are in proper form for his schooling to the gun.

Developed in this manner, besides having a knowledge most useful in the capacity of servant, he will have dash, enthusiasm, persistence and that very desirable quality commonly called "bird sense," which the dog acquires for himself, and which the trainer could not impart to him otherwise than by experience if he devoted a lifetime to it.

The foregoing contains a description of the general and essential principles employed in the development of setters and pointers in the service of the gun, and the proper theory on which to conduct their training.

Under no other conditions is it possible to develop the field trial dog; for while the imperfect field dog might give reasonable satisfaction to a shooter, the imperfect field trial dog in competition would suffer according to his imperfections.

CHAPTER IV

PUNISHMENT AND BAD METHODS

FEAR in all its forms, bird shyness (commonly called blinking), whip shyness, man shyness, gun shyness, or a shyness in taking the initiative in anything, is the common result of harshly repressive and tyrannical methods. Accordingly as the fear is associated with a particular object so one kind of shyness may be exhibited; but fear may be associated with several objects if there is cause for it from the dog's point of view. Badly treated dogs may show all the different forms, with a general apprehensiveness that something dreadful is likely to happen at any moment. Sometimes a form of shyness may result from the trainer's mistake of a moment, but generally it is the result of systematic harshness.

Whatever the cause, shyness of any kind is more or less a serious check on the dog's training,' and if it is of the kind known as blinking, it may go far toward rendering him worthless.

The trainer who succeeds best must have a genuine liking for dogs, else he is predisposed to habitual harshness or indifference. Those who have no fondness for them are rarely much of a success as skillful educators, and generally the dog which is so unfortunate as to be under their schooling has met his misfortunes of life at its very outset.

While a dog may misbehave and therefore need punishment as a preventive, it must ever be considered that there are degrees of it, times for it, and a manner of applying it which render it most effective. One trainer may whip a dog severely without thereby losing his confidence or abating his ardor; another one may give a less punishment and still evoke shyness. The one had the dog's confidence and affection ; the other had but a small part of them or none.

There are dogs which are by nature timid, but shyness is a euphemistic term for fear. When the dog is shy he is afraid. There are some painful associations of the past which he considers may become the realities of the present, and being a reasoning animal he is shy of those which suggest pain. He is afraid of the whip because it is associated with painful memories. He is afraid of his handler because the latter is a being of superior force and dangerous in certain moods. He is afraid of the gun if the concussion of it has strained and pained his ear drums, if the flash has hurt his eyes, if the smell of the foul gases has offended his delicate nose, and if he has been thrashed in a way by which he reasoned that the presence of the gun was associated with the thrashing. He is shy of birds if he is whipped concerning them before he knows for what he is whipped ; the pain then is associated with them, and when he catches scent of them he blinks. He becomes shy of taking any independent action if he is constantly nagged and balked and scolded and bedeviled, and it is a fair assumption that his master would be so if subjected to the same treatment, besides having therefrom a large fund of hard-luck stories with which to edify his friends.

While it is not possible to conduct the training of all dogs without evoking a feeling of shyness at times, it is quite possible to keep the shyness within bounds which are not harmful, if not possible to dispel the shyness as a phase of the passing moment. But if the dog's fears dominate him, his thoughts are concentrated on his own safety, and in that frame of mind he is not a promising pupil.

When a dog is trained too much, he is said to be over-trained, but this term does not properly convey the meaning of the results of over-meddling, namely, the suppression of his proper educational development and the slavish subordination of his will, which make him a mere unthinking machine in the hands of his master. By way of contrasting the difference between arrested mental development let us consider the independent action, the resourcefulness, the vigorous industry of a hound or hounds in pursuit of a fox, of greyhounds in pursuit of a jack- rabbit, of self-hunting setters and pointers when freely ranging alone through field and forest in pursuit of prey. These qualities, then at their best that is, as the dogs use them for themselves are at the degree they should be after the dog is trained to apply them in the service of the gun. But, if the trainer exercises and enforces his own judgment as to what the dog must do in every moment and every act, perpetually commanding, whistling, signaling, checking him in his every independent purpose, he will become so dominated and restricted in time that he will be a creature without a will or purpose of his own, and will look to his trainer for prompting and orders at every turn.

From the moment of the first glimmer of intelligence in the puppy till the moment he dies, he in domestication observes the domination of man. He quickly learns that man is his superior in force and knowledge, and he learns also that to him he must yield. Restrictions in working to the gun which at first were submitted to under compulsion in time are accepted by him from self-interest and habit. If the over-trained dog makes a short cast, he returns immediately for a command or signal from his trainer as to what he should do next. He roads and points perfunctorily under submission. His whole attention and acts are engrossed in the observance of his slave-hood; perpetually balked, thrashed and dominated, his ardent desire to pursue and capture in his own free and happy manner is either harmfully suppressed or entirely extinguished when he is in the company of his teacher. Such are the evils of overtraining.

A dog over-trained is of much less value as a worker than one that is but partially trained but whose natural capabilities are unimpaired. In this connection, it may be usefully remarked that practically the properly trained dog works without any orders at all. Man and dog seek with concerted action to supplement each other's efforts, working together for mutual success as a team. The dog, allowed to work in his own manner, but restricted more and more to apply his work in the service of the gun as his training progresses, in time learns that great success results from the joint efforts of his master and himself; and he then performs his part with an intelligence and a practical manipulation of means to ends far beyond any knowledge which could be conveyed to him by his teacher.

A knowledge of the evils of over-training is essential in the development and training of field dogs, but it is still more essential in respect to field trial dogs. However satisfactory to his owner an over-trained dog may be in field work, he will not be considered as even making a good showing when in competition with properly trained dogs which are performing under the critical eye of the judge. But the distinctions in respect to field and field trial training will be more fully set forth in other chapters.

Training a dog to loud orders is a bad, coarse method of teaching obedience. It is indicative of bad temper in the trainer, accomplishes nothing which could not be accomplished in a quieter way, is distinctively offensive to everyone within hearing of the hullabaloo, and gives alarming notice to all the birds in the neighborhood that a dangerous, bloodthirsty man has invaded their habitat. It thus impairs success.

Oftentimes the amateur trainer takes his gun and sets forth to kill birds, taking a green puppy along and making the education of the latter a mere inci- dent of his sport. Such is not at all training in a proper sense. It is commencing at a point which should be at a much later stage in the dog's education.

After the training has once been begun, regularity in the lessons is of prime importance. For instance, it will be conceded at once that it is much better to give a dog a half -hour lesson on each of ten days than it is to give him a lesson of five hours' duration on one day.

While a dog has very good powers of memory, he soon forgets his first lessons if he is not refreshed by daily repetition in respect to them. The trainer may have had a similar forgetfulness concerning his own first lessons, which should admonish him to be considerate.

While punishment betimes is a necessity, its use as a whole is unnecessarily comprehensive. There is no doubt that it is inflicted in most instances under a mistaken belief that it is useful in forcing a dog to learn what the trainer desires he should learn and that it really accomplishes the desired purpose. The idea, so applied, is a mistaken one. Punishment never teaches the dog anything other than in a negative manner; that is to say, it simply deters him from doing certain things. It does not in the least add to the dog's sum total of knowledge in a developmental manner. For instance, if the dog is punished for chasing a rabbit, he learns that the act has painful associations, which are likely to again recur if the act is repeated, and, expecting this, he forbears chasing. The punishment does not in the least teach him the reason why he must not chase, nor indeed anything about chasing other than that the act results in pain to himself. It is a deterrent, and he understands nothing more concerning it. On the other hand, if he had not the natural impulse and inclination, no degree of punishment would teach him how to chase a rabbit or even to chase it at all. From the dog's point of view, there is no wrong in chasing rabbit, chicken or sheep, etc. They are his natural prey; his delight in their pursuit is unbounded; he is following the natural impulses of his nature; it is his manner of obtaining the necessities of dog life; yet, if punished, he yields to superior force and desists.

There is no part of a dog's education in which punishment is of any benefit except as a corrective. The dog's knowledge increases only from experience. The trainer cannot force his own knowledge into the dog by virtue of whip or spike collar. Even when forcing a dog to retrieve with the latter instrument, its value is purely negative. It does not teach the dog anything about retrieving, as will be more fully explained in the chapter treating on that subject.

When a dog's fears are aroused, or when he is made needlessly to feel uncomfortable, worried and uneasy, his progress as a pupil is slow, If the lessons are made obnoxious to him, the trainer has succeeded in making them things to be avoided or quickly ended rather than things which have a pleasant purpose.

With a violent teacher, the dog's life is truly a sad one. His knowledge is then acquired under the most disheartening difficulties. Under similar violent conditions, the teacher as a pupil would rise in rebellion and implore the world to witness and right his wrongs. Punishment is a bad enough measure
when used as a true aid to education. It is no part of education when used to gratify anger.

Until the trainer can control his temper, if he unfortunately have one which is fiery, and fit his efforts to the dog's capacity and progress, he will be inefficient. And these corrections of himself no one can do for him other than himself. His own judgment and self-control are his only reliance, since they are personal and therefore entirely outside of the scope of any system presented by others.

CHAPTER V

THE BEST LESSONS OF PUPPYHOOD

A s INTIMATED in preceding chapters, the most useful education to the puppy is that in Nature's own school. His best development, mentally, physically, and educationally, comes from his own powers of observation and practice.

The training which in domestication he receives from association with his master, and from the more special schooling in working to the gun, is but a mere incident.

Considering his education as a whole, as the puppy develops, the trainer can do much to strengthen the ties of friendly association and to evoke therewith enthusiastic effort. If he gives the puppy a run in the fields every day or two, feeds him regularly, and joins him more or less in his plays, he becomes to the latter an object of distinguished consideration. The puppy thereby is gradually dominated and accepts his master as the one who is in authority. His consequent association of ideas, if pleasant, impels him to seek his master's society whenever his self-interest is aroused, whether in respect to wandering about through the fields, or pursuing his prey, or looking to his master for food and shelter, or enjoying the peace and comfort of mind which come from agreeable comradeship with him. By this association he forms a friendly alliance with his master, which, after a length of time, becomes a habit of life, and, if properly cherished, a true second nature.

By joining the puppy betimes in his plays, and when afield by permitting him to revel in the delights of strategic stalking and chasing young birds and butterflies, circumventing frogs and admiring and studying all Nature through the organ of scent, as his master in an analogous manner studies it through the organ of sight, he becomes way-wise, gains a knowledge of the things of the outer world, besides being afforded the freedom of action so essential to his physical development and well-being.

A puppy, when constantly on a chain or in confinement, can learn nothing of value to his master or to himself, simply because under such conditions no opportunity to learn is afforded. A case in point is that of the mature city dog which, for the first time experiencing the delights of a visit to the country, displays the most unbounded ignorance, though overflowing with amazement and ecstasy. The common domestic animals excite both his predatory interest and apprehension of danger. Even the sight of a cow in the pasture, though his instinct may impel him to make a bold front, fills him with the gravest alarms, as shown by his waverings in alert retreats and reluctant advances. Again, he romps about in a foolish manner, doing a thousand trivial or foolish things, at cross purposes with every happening, and his poor mind ever filled with wonderment.

If confined constantly, besides being ignorant, he is mentally dwarfed, physically inferior, more or less misshapen, with a soured temper and an impaired capacity for companionship. In fact, if he is kept in confinement till he matures, there is likely to be a general lifelong depreciation of his faculties and capabilities.

On the other hand, the dog which has his liberty learns the meaning of everything within his environment, and adjusts his deportment accordingly.

While permitting him to enjoy his own natural riotous manner, the ecstatic pleasure of expending surplus energy, the trainer will have no difficulty in maintaining his own domination. Many objectionable natural tendencies may be suppressed incidentally, such as an inclination to chase sheep or poultry, etc. From the puppy point of view there is no harm in pursuing them; indeed, he cannot know that they are not objects of legitimate pursuit and capture before he is so taught by experience. From his standpoint every living animal found in the woods and fields is there to be chased by him if he feels in the humor to do so, or to be killed if he wishes to compass its death.

In this connection, by considering how easily he can teach the dog to blink sheep, etc., the trainer will the better comprehend how he may unintentionally teach him to blink birds. The dog considers the immediate relation of circumstances. He, when blinking, associates some painful experience with the birds. If the painfulness be from scoldings and whippings, he quite reasonably considers that they were administered for taking notice of the birds at all rather than for flushing and chasing them, the latter being acts which, from his standpoint, are at first quite right

It thus will be noted that a certain degree of freedom and association with man is essential to the dog's best education as. a servant in the interests of the gun. Nor are all the advantages of companionship to be charged to the puppy in the matter of training. The trainer is also benefited thereby. It gives him the best of opportunities to study the puppy's peculiarities and abilities. He will note whether his pupil is intelligent or stupid, timid or bold, diligent or lazy, calm or excitable, etc. In fact, it will be a distinct gain to him if he cultivates a habit of close observation of the traits and doings of his pupils at all times.

No two dogs have precisely the same talents, nor the same methods of accomplishing their purposes. Indeed, most dogs vary widely in their powers, and the application of them. Each dog has an individuality of his own. He can best perform in his own natural manner. Nothing, therefore, will be gained by any attempts to make him work up to some ideal, even though it be the most famous ideal ever imagined. The idea of the ideal can never be communicated to the dog.

The best that the trainer can do is to make the most of the powers the dog is endowed with by Nature. This is the standard of effort. The trainer develops the puppy to the extent of his abilities, and having done that he can do no more. If the puppy has not the powers of greatness within himself, it is impossible to develop him beyond his limitations; as much so as it is to develop a man into a great orator, musician, artist, etc., if he has not the natural talents for any of these accomplishments.

As to the house training or house breaking, as it is more commonly called the puppy acquires most of it by virtue of scoldings and the broomstick. If he appreciates the best bed and bedroom for a kennel, he feels that a lashed hide, scoldings, cold looks and unfriendly surveillance are matters worth noting and heeding. When driven from the parlor at the point of the broomstick he avoids it thereafter as a place of pains and discomfort. The dining room table and the food placed upon it, by virtue of a broomstick, are conceded by him, sooner or later, to be a place for his betters. Banished repeatedly from the house in disgrace, and deprived of the friendly regard of its members for the time being, he suffers pain and deprivation, consequently his own self-interest prompts him to learn what the household regulations are, as they concern himself, what the penalty is if they are violated, and what privileges are accorded to him on the lines of the least resistance.

CHAPTER VI

YARD BREAKING

T HE preliminary schooling of the dog, commonly called yard breaking/ consists in teaching him the proper acts of obedience in response to certain commands which are of general and special utility in controlling him in his work afield and at other times. By establishing a habit of prompt and cheerful obedience to such commands before the more serious training in the work afield begins, it is readily apparent that a distinct educational gain is made. Incidentally, these preliminary lessons, by the opportunities of companionship which they afford, establish the friendliest relations between teacher and pupil, if they are kindly and sympathetically conducted.

From his hours of play, wherein the puppy frisks and frolics as he pleases, hardly any fatigue ensues. He then is following the simple impulses of his own mind, which do not cause great nervous strain, over- heating, confusion, or intense worry. He abhors lessons which are devoid of all amusement. If they are gently and amusingly given success is more progressive. After a time mental strength and stamina will develop, and then longer lessons may be given without distressing him.

Later in the training the powers of his mind become so much more vigorous that the most difficult of the training lessons are learned with greater ease than were the far more simple beginnings.

To concentrate his mind on what is being taught him in the first lessons is exceedingly difficult and fatiguing to him ; therefore the teacher would better set a short limit to the lessons, say fifteen or twenty minutes. He also should avoid the habit of constantly bossing and nagging the pupil between lessons. If he is bossed and bullied incessantly, he, after a time, loses all power of independent initiative, and is so dominated by his tutor that he is a mere unthinking machine.

These suggestions as to over discipline are quite as applicable when the dog is receiving his experience on game as they are when he is receiving his yard breaking. His subjugation to the entire domination of his trainer is undesirable at any time. Yet many good dogs are annually spoiled, or their best efforts marred, by rigidly restricting them to lines of action in their yard training which are mistakenly deemed to be the correct thing when they are actually working to the gun.

While the trainer may have in mind the nice manner in which the theoretical training will fit into the practical work, the dog is entirely ignorant that it is training, or, indeed, that it has any reference to anything at all useful. He recognizes that he is cramped and confined in his efforts, and, if so mentally enslaved till it becomes a habit, he exhibits slavish deference at all times.

Without the ability or inclination to hunt game, the dog is worthless for field purposes. Some dogs, if checked too much, perceive nothing which appeals to their self-interest, and consequently they lose all inclination to search for birds. If the dog refuses to hunt it is beyond the power of any one to force him to do so.

This is a point which the trainer should ever bear in mind that is to say, it is the dog's self-interest which impels him to seek game. If this self-interest is not preserved all incentive to effort on the dog's part is gone. His natural impulse for the pursuit of birds and his enthusiasm in his efforts to capture them are so great that he will submit to much balking and punishment before he will desist ; but there is a certain limit beyond which he will net maintain interest and effort if the trainer is over-restrictive.

In the yard training, as in the field work, the trainer should teach and handle quietly. Turbulence in most instances denotes ill-temper or a badly disciplined mind. The loud and incessant issuing of commands and blowing of whistles, in season and cut of season, with or without cause, are faults common to nearly all amateurs, and for that matter to nearly all professionals. The majority of trainers are self-taught, so that bad habits of method and manner acquired in the beginning are likely to be retained by them throughout their lives. Habituated thoroughly to their own ways, they often are quite unconscious of the hullabaloo which they create, and of their offensiveness to such company as may be with them, to say nothing of the great handicap which they impose upon any dog which may be under their control.

Boisterous shouting of orders and constant whistling are the cause of many flushes. If the frightened birds be in the proximity of the dog at the time, the noisy trainer is prone to consider that the dog is at fault rather than himself, who s really the guilty party. When so noisily intent on securing obedience in an habitual hullabaloo manner, the trainer is generally lost to all incidental happenings, so far as they relate to his own faults.

It is not at all difficult to teach a dog obedience to quiet commands and gentle signals, and it is infinitely better to handle him in that manner afield than in a manner of noise and violence, apart from all considerations of ease and elegance.

While being taught, the dog quickly learns the signs which indicate punishment and the signs which indicate that the teacher is pleased or displeased. Changes of voice and expression of countenance, whether of pleasure or irritation, are noted and correctly interpreted. It is therefore essential for the best progress in the lessons that the teacher preserve an equable exterior and action at all times, be he pleased or displeased.

In the summer days it is better to give the lessons in the early morning and evening, the temperature then being coolest. When the puppy is warm and panting he suffers much discomfort, and it is then difficult to. hold his interest or attention.

His mind, being immature and undisciplined, can compass only the simplest details. Therefore it is best to begin with the most elementary lessons, and thus his ideas will be developed in a natural manner, and obedience will be enforced without breaking his spirit or lessening his self-confidence. As with the child in its first attempts at learning, so it is with the puppy; it is extremely difficult and wearisome for it to at first understand the simplest teachings or concentrate its mind on any subject which requires thought. Under such circumstances, the amateur teacher should not too hastily, assume that the puppy is stupid.

When teaching the first lessons it is better to be within a room or yard from which he cannot escape, even if so inclined. Undoubtedly he will make many attempts to do so. It is good training to permit him to make such attempts with the resultant failures. Then, after repeated disappointments, he will abandon them.

If the trainer commands the puppy to do something under such circumstances that obedience can- not be enforced, and the latter then escapes or succeeds in disobeying, a very troublesome factor is thereby introduced. The advantages of disobedience are quickly learned and remembered, and thereafter, when he is disinclined to obedience, if pressed to a degree which is displeasing to him, he runs away.

In this connection it may be remarked that every precaution should be taken to prevent the puppy from running away, for once he learns that he can escape, the difficulties of reducing him to subjection are many times multiplied. This alone suggests the wisdom of refraining from any attempts at training between lessons in places where the puppy is not confined within walls or fences.

The lesson should end with some play and romping by teacher and pupil, so that there may be pleasant associations referring to it, in the mind of the latter at least.

The commands to which obedience may be taught in the yard lessons are as follows:

"GO"

The command "Go on' 5 denotes that the dog is to start freely forward and work according to his own or master's pleasure. During the early months of the pupil's puppyhood this command may be easily taught. It is readily accomplished by associating it with the act of freeing the puppy from his kennel, or uttering it at the moment of freeing him from the chain or lead strap when he is taken afield.

When so freed from either chain or kennel, he would *""go on" whether the command were uttered or not, and this is the main reason that it is so easily taught when the pupil is still a tender puppy. It then is in entire consonance with his inclination, and "he learns readily its import by associating it with freedom from all restraint.

A motion of the hand forward, associated with it, is soon understood as signifying the same as the order, and is quite as promptly acted upon.

If the puppy has any spirit at all he takes unbounded pleasure on hearing the command "Go on," or en seeing the signal, either of which denotes that he is at liberty to romp at his own free will.

"COME IN."

"Come in" denotes that the pupil is to cease all effort other than coming promptly and directly to his master. It is not so easily taught as "Go on," for the reason that it nearly always runs counter to the pupil's inclination. He is rarely inclined to give up the pleasures of free romping or other interesting purposes in which he may be engaged at the time he hears the order; therefore it in most instances is necessary to apply force to establish the desired obedience. Nevertheless, force should not be used till the puppy is properly matured and the formal yard training begins, inasmuch as it does not matter whether the puppy obeys promptly or not before that time.

When the proper juncture arrives it is necessary to enforce the most thorough obedience to this command; otherwise no progress worthy of any consideration can be made in any branch of training.

No reluctant, hesitating or slovenly obedience should be tolerated. It is one of the easiest commands to teach if the trainer is properly persistent and methodical, and yet there are few orders more commonly disobeyed or evaded.

Pronounced obstinacy or disobedience must be corrected by force. It should be impressed upon the puppy that obedience to the order is uncompromisingly imperative; that nothing is left to his own inclination in this matter other than prompt obedience. The discipline established thereby in this one branch has a beneficent effect on all other branches of the training, since it establishes a general domination of the teacher. A disregard of this order denotes that the dog is under little control in any respect.

The spike collar is the best instrument when the application of force is necessary. The description and uses of it, set forth in another chapter, should be read and carefully noted. It will accomplish the most desirable results when used in the parts of the dog's education to which it is applicable; but, on the other hand, there is no instrument more harmful or capable of more brutal action than is the spike collar when improperly applied.

The advantages of the collar when used to force the dog to "Come on" are that it inflicts pain upon him at the time and place that he is guilty of disobedience.

If he is standing at a distance from his handler he thereby

has no immunity from punishment when the collar is on his neck. It forces him to come in, however much he may struggle against it. In the meantime, the trainer need not make any alarming demonstration, it being quite different from the portentously hostile actions inseparable from the use of the whip. The force is so directly and promptly applied that the pupil associates it entirely with the act of disobedience.

The whip is not even remotely a substitute for the collar in teaching this order. If the puppy comes in and is whipped, he observes that punishment is the result. He soon shows reluctance in coming in when there are grounds to suspect a whipping. On the other hand, the collar forces him to obey, and then punishment ceases. If the trainer then caresses him, thereby indicating that he has done quite right, he quickly learns that obedience results in that which is pleasurable instead of that which is painful.

The collar punishes the dog when he is in the act of disobedience; the whip punishes after he has obeyed. Besides being promptly effective in establishing obedience, the collar is permanent in its effect.

The manner of applying the collar is simple. It is put on the puppy's neck, with twenty or thirty yards of strong, light cord attached to it. The trainer, holding the end of the cord in his hand, and the pupil being any number of yards away within the compass of the cord, quietly gives the order and pulls in the dog at the same time. The latter, in all probability, struggles and attempts to run away, or furiously he may attempt to fight the collar. In any case, the trainer holds him steadily till his flurry is over. He soon becomes convinced that on his part the attempt to meet force with force is futile and painful.

No attempt at schooling should be made till the dog ceases struggling and is reconciled to yield to the force of the collar. This may require two or three minutes, or two or three lessons, according to the circumstances of the case. When he accepts the cellar peacefully, give the command "Come in," and pull him in within reach of the hand, so that he may be petted and caressed till he has recovered his self-confidence and composure. The trainer next walks away repeats the order, and pulls the dog in again if he disobeys.

He soon notes that the punishment is most likely to occur when he is away from his handler, and will endeavor to follow him closely about as he walks away. This anticipation of the order may be guarded against by fastening a wooden or iron pin to the cord four or five feet from the collar and sticking it in the ground. The trainer then walks away, waits a few moments, gives the order calmly, at the same time pulling on the cord, which in turn pulls the pin out of the ground, thereby permitting the dog to come in promptly if he will do so, or, otherwise, forcing him to come in.

These lessons should be repeated till he will come in promptly to the order. Next, in a room or yard from which he cannot escape, he may be drilled without the collar. If he disobeys, it is put on him, and the forcing process is repeated. The lessons are repeated till he will obey from habit.

In the field he will need much further disciplining in this as in other branches of his education, as the temptation to act independently is a great incentive to disobedience.

A proper composure and deliberation on the part of the trainer add greatly to the efficacy of the lessons. Hurry and senseless violence do much to retard progress in this as in all other branches of the dog's education.

A long blast on the whistle is commonly used to denote the same act as the command, and it is taught in precisely the same manner.

Notwithstanding the ease and thoroughness with Avhich "Come in" may be taught, there are few dogs which are properly proficient in it. At field trials, in particular, the place where one would expect to find the greatest perfection in matters of obedience, it not infrequently happens that the trainer engages in a laborious task when he attempts to bring a dog in during a heat or at other times. Some field trial handlers find it necessary to keep their dogs on chain to prevent them from breaking away when they desire them to cease work. All this shows rank neglect of the proper discipline from a field point of view, though it has for a purpose the encouragement of the dog to remain out at his work when in competition, regardless of the whistling or ordering indulged in by a*n opposing handler. The handlers* of such dogs, independent of competitive consideration, are generally satisfied to control them in any kind of slipshod manner rather than to take the more troublesome and efficient method of teaching the command specially till it is thoroughly inculcated as a matter of obedience.

CHAPTER VII

"HEEL"

The order commonly used to denote that the dog is to follow behind the shooter is "Heel". There are constantly recurring occasions for its use, such as to keep the dog from aimlessly and annoyingly running about; to save him from expending his strength in working out unfavorable or barren ground; to prevent him while in town or country from intrusive visitations to yards and houses while passing them, and to keep him generally in place when the shooter desires that he stop hunting.

Special pains should be taken to teach perfect obedience to this order, as it is essential to the best control of the dog at all times, and it is particularly useful when two or more dogs are to be handled afield together.

The proper obedience to this command is not established till the dog will come promptly to heel when ordered, and there remain reliably and quietly till he receives the order or signal to go on, and all this whether the eye of the trainer is on him or not. Restraining the dog at heel betimes rests him without any lessening of the day's sport. It also serves as a protection to him from the attacks of vicious curs, and from frittering away his time in visiting other curs of social proclivities.

Simple as is the act required in response to this order, and notwithstanding the ease with which it can be taught, few dogs are trained to obey it with even a reasonable degree of observance. Commonly as taught the dog comes dawdling in with contemptuous castings to the right and left, nosing about meanwhile, and, when he at last is at heel, if the trainer takes his eyes oft" him for a moment, he casts back to the rear, begins hunting in the wake of his trainer, paying visits to vagrant curs, or pottering about in search of bones and garbage. A whipping is a great benefit to the offender in such instances.

The first lessons in teaching this command may be given in the yard, or when taking him for a run in the fields. It is better to lead him with a cord which is held in one hand while the other hand holds a whip.

At first he will go anywhere rather than behind his trainer, and may exhibit more or less obstinacy and resistance if his inclination is opposed. When walking alone, the command "Heel" is given, at the same time jerking him toward the rear with the cord. If he, after being forced to the rear, attempts to go ahead of his trainer, he should be whipped back to place, the trainer being careful to so hit him that he will endeavor to get behind for safety. Then the trainer calmly resumes his walk, and any further attempts to lag behind or to force ahead are to be thwarted as at first.

If he is resolutely obstinate and resistant, a spike collar should be put on him. Then if he charges ahead or sags in the collar in a refusal to go at all, or if he struggles to escape, a pull on the cord will correct him and bring him into place at once. If he is persistent in charging ahead, a sharp cut or two with the whip will make him retreat to his place in the rear.

At every correction the command should be repeated so that he will learn to associate it with the act of taking his place at the heels of the trainer. This should be persisted in till he will walk steadily at heel. However, no more punishment should be inflicted than is really needed to enforce the command. Regular repetition of the lessons and fidelity in enforcing obedience to details should be relied upon to teach steadiness rather than violence, long lessons and hurry.

That is the first stage. When the cord and collar are removed he may immediately attempt to exercise is own pleasure. He must then be taught that no liberties will be tolerated, whether the cord restrains him or not. The trainer should keep a close eye on him, and if he dawdles behind, or attempts to break away to the rear, he should be forced to return to his proper place, punishment being given according to his needs. Nothing short of implicit obedience to orders should be accepted. If, from the beginning, he feels that the eye of the trainer is upon him, he will soon cease to take liberties which violate orders.

On the other hand, he should not be kept so continuously at heel that he becomes habituated to it, or acquires a liking for it. If he is of a lazy disposition, or easily wearied, he quickly learns that he can have greater comfort at his master's heels than any to be found elsewhere.

After a time the discipline will be firmly inculcated and habitual. Then, whether the trainer is afoot, horseback or in a wagon, the dog will reliably and cheerfully follow behind when ordered to do so.

The advantage of obedience to the command is especially advantageous when two dogs are used at the same time afield. The ability to keep one dog at heel in a trained way while the other is working is a material advantage in many ways; it affords an opportunity to rest one dog while the other is at work; it is a means of quietly restraining one dog when interference with the other is undesirable, as in roading, drawing, pointing, etc. ; and it has a general moral effect by keeping the dog in proper restraint when he is not engaged in the work at hand.

When a dog is to be worked in company with other dogs, it is well to teach him to go on from heel by merely speaking his name. Thus, if the two dogs A and B are at heel, and the trainer wishes the former to begin work, he utters the name of A, looking him in the eye at the same time. If B starts also, which he is quite likely to do at first, he must instantly be brought back to heel and kept there till the trainer orders him out. In time each dog will learn that when he hears his name uttered, when at heel, it is the same as the order "Go on."

When the order is thoroughly inculcated, the trainer can take his dogs along following at heel, and send out with perfect ease any dog that he wishes to send.

"DROP" or "DOWN CHARGE."

"Drop" or "Down Charge" or "Charge" are terms commonly used to signify that the dog is to lie down, and so remain till ordered up. The manner of teaching obedience to it is very simple. A cord, four or five feet long, is tied to the dog's collar. The trainer holds the end of it in one hand while with the other he forces the dog to lie down, at the same time uttering the command "Drop." A tap or two on the shoulder is given with a whip if he attempts to rise. After a time he is permitted to rise and the lesson is then repeated.

After a few lessons he will understand the meaning of the order, but may be disinclined to obey it. Under such circumstances the trainer holds the end of the cord in one hand and utters the. order, at the same time hitting the dog sharply on the shoulder with the whip. He will soon drop, and punishment should then cease instantly. If he rolls over on his back, a position which is entirely undesirable, a few light taps with the whip on his paws or chest will cause him to turn quickly over in the right position. This is kept up day after day till the pupil will drop promptly to the order.

If the trainer desires to teach him to drop to signal, he raises his right hand in the air when he gives the order, so that the dog associates it with the command. If the signal alone is used at any time and the dog disobeys it, obedience to it is taught in manner precisely the same as in teaching the oral order.

When the order is given nothing less than instant obedience should be accepted. No nosing about, seeking for a good place in which to lie down, or other evasions of any kind, should be tolerated. The place where the dog stood at the time of the command should be the place where he should drop.

Some special lessons in the open field are necessary to make him reliably obedient therein. A strong wooden pin should be firmly driven into the ground, and to it the dog is tied, leaving him with twenty or thirty yards of free cord. He is then made to drop close by the pin. The trainer then walks away, and if the dog follows he is taken back to place, forced to drop and properly admonished. If he attempts to bolt, the cord will check him.

If, however, he resolutely persists in his attempts to bolt, a spike collar may be put on him, and after he is snubbed by it once or twice he will desist from his attempts to escape.

He is taught to drop to shot by discharging a gun or pistol and forcing him to drop to the report precisely as if it were the word of command. A pistol with a light powder charge is most commonly used to teach him this branch. Great care should be exercised to avoid causing gun-shyness, and no attempt should be made to teach dropping to shot till the dog is thoroughly without fear of the gun. However, the act of dropping to shot is of no special utility.

Dropping to wing may be classed as another over-refinement. It has no special advantages, and has many distinct disadvantages. It is taught by making him drop to wing every time that a bird flushes within hearing or sight of him, and after a time by adding thereto some mild punishment if he is slow to understand or reluctant to obey. However, in this respect the amateur would best make haste slowly, very slowly, for he may by indirect punishment make the dog afraid of the bird, if its rise is associated with too much pain. Herein lies the cause in many instances of the serious fault called "blinking."

"Hold up" is the order commonly used when the trainer desires the dog to rise from the "Drop." As it is in accord with his inclination in most instances, it is quite as easily taught as the order "Go on." A signal of the hand, accompanying the order, is understood by the puppy after he observes it a sufficient number of times. However, if he should happen to be of a sulky, malicious nature, and consequently reluctant to obey, the spike collar may be used to enforce obedience. It is placed on his neck, with a strong piece of rope attached to it. The trainer gives the order "Hold up," and if the dog refuses to obey, a light jerk on the collar or a repetition of light jerks will quickly bring him to his feet. This lesson repeated a few times will insure prompt and permanent obedience.

"TOHO."

"Toho" is the order which signifies that the dog is to stop and stand still, much after the same manner that a horse is supposed to respond to the order "Whoa," though, unlike the latter, it is of no practical use. This command, if properly taught, requires a great deal of pains and labor on the part of the trainer, besides cumbering the mind of the pupil with a term and its significance having no useful purpose or application in practical field work. Theoretically, from an extremely superficial point of view, as the dog stands still when he points game, there would seem to be a most useful gain in furthering the act of pointing and backing by teaching him to stop and stand still at the word of command. In practice, teaching the term and enforcing obedience to it retard rather than advance the training of the dog.

However, the older writers earnestly set forth its importance as an essential to the dog's proper education, and made much of it accordingly. It was considered useful in teaching both pointing and backing, besides being of spectacular interest at almost any time that the dog was engaged in serious work. When he was feathering near the game on which he was roading or drawing, and the sharp command

"Toho" caused him to stop and stand still, it was

considered that the act came near to being a point and was therefore of material assistance in teaching the real point. On the theory that the trainer teaches the dog to point, is was not inconsistent therewith, but when we consider that the trainer does not teach the dog to point, and, furthermore, cannot so teach him, the uselessness of "Toho" is at once apparent. Nevertheless, as it was consistent with the old theories, it served a useful purpose for the older authors, who were not so intent on words to express true knowledge as they were on words to fill a book.

"Toho" is a most difficult order to teach thoroughly, and still more difficult to enforce afield after it is taught. If the trainer disregards all else pertaining to training and makes a specialty of educating the dogs to obey "Toho," by the time he has accomplished it he will have spent much more time and many times more effort than would be required to establish correct backing and pointing without it. Under it teacher and pupil are in a manner slaves to a worthless idea.

After it is taught, with much labor and pains, there is but little opportunity to use it after the manner set forth in the older books, for out of the sum total of opportunities presented to the dog to point birds, the trainer concerning them is in profound ignorance of the proper juncture of time and place at which to order the dog to "Toho." To apply the order intelligently, the trainer must know the time and place at which the dog should make his stand, yet ordinarily he does not know where the birds are, or, indeed, whether there are any at all. If by any chance the trainer sees the birds, he seldom is able to get the dog in the right position to fit the order; but even if he succeeds in getting him to the right place, his own sight and judgment are in no sense a substitute for the dog's sense of smell and consciousness.

The meddlesome attempt to force the dog to proceed according to the trainer's thought and plans, with the incidental bawlings of "Toho, toho," etc., seldom fails to flush the birds and confuse the dog. DOG

Conditions which make all clear to the trainer's sense of sight may not conditions which do not in the least serve the dog's sense of smell. If the dog stops to the order without having scent of the birds, it is a meaningless act so far as pointing is concerned, and if he stops to order when he has scent of them, it has no more significance of a point than if the trainer attempted to do the pointing him-self. Ordinarily, when on birds, the puppy pays no more attention to the command "Toho" than he does to the murmur of the gentle breezes. If, then, there is a warfare over the disobedience it is obstructive to his best advancement.

If obedience is at length pounded into him and there is no other manner of enforcing it in this connection interest in the birds is incidentally pounded out of him.

Nevertheless, some of the old school will stoutly maintain that dogs are beneficially assisted to point by the aid of "Toho," although dogs, as a matter of fact, have learned to point and back in spite of it.

Punishment in reference to birds is the source of blinking. Even for the benefits advocated for "Toho" the

"Drop" fulfills all requirements. Let us assume that the handler, for any good reason, desires the dog to stop when reading. He gives the command or signal to "Drop," and the dog ceases at once. Being down he cannot sneak forward, as he can when standing up. In either instance, by obedience to the order, the dog's mind is diverted from his work, and the handler engages his attention instead. This will be more apparent by referring to the chapter on pointing, backing, etc., in this work.

If the trainer, nevertheless, desires to teach it, it can be made a part of the yard training, and is best done in a room or small enclosure. The trainer ties a cord to the dog's collar and walks him around, giving betimes the command "Toho," and incidentally therewith forcing him to stand still. After he stands a reasonable length of time, the trainer utters the command "Go on," or "Hie on," and then the walk is resumed.

Lessons in this manner should be conducted day after day till the pupil has a comprehension of the command, and after he shows some obedience to it he may be trained to stop on his dinner or pieces of food.

A piece of meat may be thrown out. As he rushes eagerly for it he is ordered to "Toho." He refuses to obey, as a matter of course, and the cord in the trainer's hand checks him and prevents him from seizing the meat. He is forced to stand still, notwithstanding his eagerness, and after a time he is ordered on and permitted to eat the morsel. At his regular meals he may have a similar training.

These lessons are persisted in till at length the dog will stop promptly and reliably at the command or signal as the trainer may desire. He can be taught so thoroughly that he will stop to order at every step as he advances to the dish containing his food, and can be held on the

"Toho" with his nose on the food. But stopping to order on food bears no relation to a point or the purposes of a point, although it may be considered as something out of the ordinary in the way of a trick.

The arm extended at less than a right angle from the body is supposed to be the best signal to designate "Toho."

ADMONITORY ORDERS
"Hi" and "Ware" are exclamations which as the trainer choose may be used as a warning for the dog to desist from undesirable acts in which he is engaged, or to attract his attention to a signal. Those consisting of a single word are best.

IRREGULAR COMMANDS
Long commands, such as "Come here to me, I tell you," "Look out," "What are you about?" "Why don't you hunt out that corner, you fool?" etc., should be avoided if it is within the power of the trainer to do so. However, if he must prattle or perish, it is better to prattle, notwithstanding that it is detrimental to the dog's best service.

The notes of the whistle or signals used to denote certain commands, and no others, should be used invariably, and thus they will always have a fixed and definite meaning.

Sometimes the beginner, when the dog is on birds or seeking for them, will deliver a continued discourse mostly devoted to the dog's utter worthlessness, notwithstanding that the dog is but a few months old, and a novice in respect to what is correct methods or wrong methods.

Having taught the puppy the meaning of the orders "Come in" and "Go on" as the first lessons, the further special yard training may profitably rest in abeyance until the puppy is eight or ten months old, or a year old for that matter. Under proper conditions he then begins to have some maturity of ideas, has become way wise, if he has had proper treatment and freedom, and thus from his own perception will intelligently adjust his actions to the governing circumstances of his life.

In teaching these commands, one thing at a time should be the rule. By observing it, the puppy will be much more thoroughly taught, and with infinitely less confusion to him than if several educationary branches are all attempted at the same time.

"Fetch" and "Seek" are commands which are applicable when the dog is desired to retrieve, and will be treated fully under that head.

CHAPTER VIII

POINTING

T HE pointing instinct, possessed and exhibited by nearly all setters and pointers, is a conspicuous characteristic of their methods in capturing "their prey. Contrary to what is commonly maintained, it has no natural reference whatever to the service of mankind.

Man observes that he can usefully apply the pointing trait to his own profit, and he utilizes it accordingly. In like manner he utilizes the powerful horse as a beast of burden ; his speed for purposes of rapid transportation; his hide for good leather; yet all these properties were originally for the horse's own benefit.

The ability to point well is essential to the existence of the dog when in a wild state, since it is a material aid to him in the struggle for existence. In domesticity, he does not lose the instinctive desire to pursue and capture prey. He, like man, has the hunting instinct strongly present, notwithstanding the centuries of domestication. He easily reverts to a wild state, utilizing then for his own preservation the powers and methods which man rather egotistically avers were implanted in him for the benefit of man himself.

Man can neither force nor induce a dog to seek birds if the latter refuses to do so; and he does so when there is nothing left which appeals to his self-interest.

His involuntary efforts, exhibited when in search of prey, man restricts within certain limits to his own service, and thereby appropriates to himself the fruits of the dog's labors. And herein is where many old and new writers have erred in their inferences. They observed that the dog could be so trained that man was the beneficiary of his work, and they rather illogically deduced that therefore the instinct was acquired for the benefit of mankind.

When a dog, with more or less rigidity of posture. stops to the scent of game or prey, the act is called pointing, setting or standing. It is observed in a more or less rudimentary state in all dogs which are used for hunting purposes, and is sometimes exhibited even by curs which have no pretensions whatever to good breeding, or, for that matter, to any breeding at all.

The following excerpt from Stonehenge has furnished nearly all writers their data for the origin of the pointing instinct: "The setter is, without doubt, either descended from the spaniel, or both are off- hoots from the same parent stock. Originally that is, before the improvements in the gun introduced the practice of 'shooting flying' it is believed that he was merely a spaniel taught to 'stop' or 'set' as soon as he came upon the scent of the partridge, when a net was drawn over the covey by two men. Hence he was made to drop close to the ground, an attitude which is now unnecessary, though it is taught by some breakers, and notably to fast dogs, who could not otherwise stop themselves quickly enough to avoid flushing. Manifestly, a dog prone on the ground allowed the net to be drawn over him better than if he were standing up ; an4 hence the former attitude was preferred, an additional reason for its adoption being, probably, that it was more easily taught to a dog like the spaniel, which has not the natural cataleptic attitude of the pointer. But when 'shooting flying' came in vogue, breakers made canine attempt to assimilate the attitude of the setting spaniel or 'setter/ as he was now called to that of the pointer ; and in process of time, and possibly also by crossing with that dog, they succeeded, though even after the lapse of more than a century the cataleptic condition is not as fully displayed by the setter as by the pointer."

It would be difficult to crowd into the same amount of space more trashy nonsense than is contained in the foregoing quotation, and yet it has served writers for generations as good warrant for asserting as fact what it merely presents as probabilities.

Modern writers do not hesitate to assert that the setter is derived from the spaniel, though Stonehenge qualifies it by stating: "Or both are offshoots from the same parent stock." In plain words, he did not know what they were derived from. Again, it is much easier to evolve the dropping attitude from the point than it was to evolve from the point the dropping attitude. The instinct which, moreover, is conceded to have been natural to the pointer has a farfetched theory most laboriously worked out to explain its existence in the setter. Why it should be natural to the one and not to the other, Stonehenge leaves it to the reader to solve as best he can.

He also treats the point as being cataleptic, and advances that trait as a reason why it was necessary to make the setter drop when the net was thrown over him. The point is neither cataleptic nor remotely related to the cataleptic state. The pointing dog is keenly alert in every faculty. His eyes glow, his nostrils play as they inhale the scent, his judgment gauges the place and distance of the prey, and his muscles are tense and ready for instant action in the quick, powerful strike to seize and hold.

It also is extraordinary that "fast dogs, who could not otherwise stop themselves quickly enough to avoid flushing," could stop and drop, a much more difficult feat than it is to stop and stand still. It is not at all difficult for a fast dog to check himself at full speed. It is extremely rare, indeed, when it is necessary for him to stop instantly. In most instances he catches the scent and proceeds to locate,

Any cur of good hunting instinct and ability may be taught to hunt and point birds with more or less success. In the course of time he learns that capture in the pursuit of birds is consequent to silent and careful effort only, though the point work of the cur is inefficient and unreliable from a point of utility as compared with that of the pointer and setter.

The pause to capture, called pointing, is a mere incident in the exercise of the general purpose. It may have even a wider application, as exhibited by hounds or curs which have been trained to road and stop on deer, keeping close in front of the deer hunter while so roading and drawing, and timing their efforts with exquisite judgment for the success of the gun.

Strange dogs, meeting on the highway for the first time, not infrequently stiffen and feather as they stealthily draw toward each other, mimicking am- bush and attack, or preparing for actual battle, ac- cording to their whims or the governing circumstances. The uses of pointing, as exercised in the dog's activities, comprehend a much greater scope than that considered by sportsmen. Setters and pointers, as a matter of reason, employ distinct methods in the pursuit of fur and feather. When in the pursuit of rabbits, they are openly vigorous and dashing, give tongue merrily, and pay no heed to cautious effort. When the rabbit is afoot they trust largely to their swiftness and endurance to effect a capture. On the other hand, if the rabbit is lying concealed they endeavor to compass his capture by craft, much after the method employed on birds. When in the pursuit of birds they are silent, painstakingly cautious, and tense from uncertainty. They draw then as closely as possible before making the final pause and spring to surprise and capture.

These different methods are a necessity from the different circumstances governing the different cases. They are self-evident when we consider that the rabbit must remain on the earth's surface; that it leaves a trail of scent, which is ever a clue for its pursuer to follow; and that the battle cries of the latter so alarm and confuse it that its capture is made easier thereby. On the other hand, the birds, having wings, must not be alarmed at all if a capture is to be effected, for alarm is equivalent to escape. It thus is clear that the different methods employed are imposed necessarily from the circumstances of the case. Nor are these peculiarities of method employed solely by the dog. Foxes draw on rabbits and grouse in a similar manner. Cats have an analogous manner of drawing on birds and vermin; indeed, as they often venture the attempt to capture birds in the most open places, they exhibit even greater degrees of craft and caution.

We may safely conclude that as it is a natural trait of the pointer, it therefore is an equally natural trait of the setter, as it also is more or less a trait of all other dogs and animals which seek birds and small animals as prey.

Not infrequently the pointing instinct is exhibited at a very early age, and in rare instances it is dormant past the age of maturity. Usually young puppies are profoundly affected by the scent of game birds or the sight of other birds. On the latter they will draw and point by sight, springing after and chasing them the moment that they take wing. At first, under the stimulus of their purpose, they rush heedlessly in to capture, and failing it they chase senselessly and riotously.

Failure develops great caution. As they grow older they use their noses more and exercise greater craft. As to methods, they vary; they are deter- mined by the intelligence and idiosyncrasies of the individual.

A precocious display of pointing does not in the least indicate that the puppy making it is superior to his fellows, for it requires no high degree of mental or physical ability to stand on a point. The act, moreover, may be done foolishly and aimlessly, as any other act may be done.

The nose of the dog requires a certain degree of training to become a discriminating organ of scent. Skill in its use therefore comes from experience. Commonly the first efforts of puppies at pointing are awkward and inefficient.

Different kinds of effort are indicated by certain scents, as the body scent and the foot scent, and by different degrees of intensity of the same scent. The best manner of following the scent, wind and character of the ground considered, is also an important factor. If the dog presses too closely on the birds he flushes them ;*if he stops too far away from them he is outside of the limits wherein he can make a successful spring, and therewith a reasonably successful attempt at capturing them. If he runs about over the trail aimlessly or potters to and fro, the birds may run entirely away from him.

Errors in the first attempt are to be expected. The dog learns methods only by his successes and failures. After a time his judgment and functional powers of nose become so developed and trained that he can discriminate between the body scent and the foot scent, and when pointing can estimate with precision the whereabouts of the concealed birds.

The purpose of the point, is twofold; the dog when set endeavors to accurately locate the birds by his powers of scent, and he then is in a better position to spring vigorously to capture. When he makes his point every muscle is at its utmost tension. The opening and closing jaw regulates the intake of air so that the nostrils will not be disturbed in their act of nice discrimination; the eyes are set with a fixed, bloody purpose. He may determine in an instant the whereabouts of the birds, or it may take him some moments. When he is satisfied that he has them located he springs in with astonishing energy and quickness, and many times is successful in capturing before the birds can take wing, or, taking wing, he may capture before they can get beyond his reach.

He can spring a few feet before a bird can rise from the ground a like distance. He makes many mis- takes nevertheless. Sometimes, through eddies of wind or bad judgment, he may jump in the wrong direction, or he may make his stand too far away from the birds and when he makes his spring he falls far short of reaching them, etc. Dogs in this respect vary greatly in skill.

The points of the dog, as they are naturally made in furtherance of his own purposes, as shown when he is not trained or but half trained, have a vigor and intensity which are much greater than those of the trained dog. In time the points of the latter gradually become more or less perfunctory. He learns that he must not spring forward to capture, and that therefore there is no need to set himself rigidly for it He may even become slouchy on point, and some dogs learn to lie down instead of standing up, as a dog on point naturally should do.

All dogs, however, which lie down on point do not do so as a matter of ease or indifference. Some do so as a matter of education; others as a matter of caution, sneaking forward very close to the ground when on trail, and dropping to the ground betimes for the purpose of concealment, something after the manner in which cats stalk their prey. Their alertness in playing to the gun is not diminished by being deprived of the pleasure of springing to capture; they are intent on intelligently assisting the success of the gun, and by being instrumental in the capture their self-interest is preserved.

The trainer, diverting the dog's efforts in seeking game, preserves as much as possible all the dog's pointing methods up to the juncture whereat he has located the birds, stands to collect himself and is ready to spring in, to flush and capture.

The flush and capture are all that the dog is taught to forego. The point is useful to the shooter; the flush is not. Therefore the dog is indulged in the exercise of his own self-interest in so far as permitting him to find and point birds; further than that he may not go without offense.

As mentioned hereinbefore, the dog in his first attempt should be permitted to seek and point and flush in his own manner, the trainer exercising some judgment as to how much experience is necessary to bring him to the proper stage for training to the gun.

The matter of whether the dog is headstrong or timid, or quick or slow to learn, or whether the opportunities are meager or abundant, etc., is for the exercise of the trainer's judgment. There is no arbitrary rule to determine it.

When the proper time arrives for steadying the puppy on point, if he flushes he is brought back to the place where he should have pointed and there is forced to remain till he recovers from his excitement and foregoes his purpose. As the flush is repeated opportunity after opportunity, the trainer evinces more and more disapproval by scoldings and more or less punishment, according to the requirements of the case.

At length, when the puppy has been taught what is required of him, if he springs in and flushes he is more severely punished. As to how much punishment is necessary the trainer must exercise some nice judgment. Some dogs require very little ; others require a great deal of punishment. In time, the dog observes that the gun is a powerful adjunct, and he works to it intelligently to obtain the greater advantages of co-operation.

The trainer is most likely to err in hurrying too much. He is anxious to have the puppy pointing at once, and he is apt to use the whip too soon and too often in consequence.

There is, in this connection, a certain difficulty in making the dog understand that the pursuit of the birds is not for his own benefit; that he is to stop short where his every natural impulse is to go on and that punishment has reference to steady pointing and thus to the interests of the shooter.

By injudicious punishment the dog may mistakenly understand that he has done wrong in finding the birds at all, and thereafter when near birds he may shy away from and quietly leave them so as to avoid the war which is likely to ensue if he happens to flush them. This act is called blinking, and is about the worst fault that a dog can have. Not infrequently weeks are required to cure it, and the trainer who was the cause of it, from the fear he inspires in the pupils, is unable to cure it. A change of trainers is therefore then necessary. This alone should make clear the need of proper deliberation in training the dog to stanchness on point.

Excessive violence defeats its own ends. The dog cannot be taught to point if he has no inclination to do so. The instinct is slow, to develop in some dogs. be latent for one or two years. If the dog has good capabilities otherwise, he should not be condemned because he is disinclined to point in his puppyhood.

The self-interest of the dog may be excited by acts which are pleasurable or profitable, or both combined. Seeking birds is such an enthralling passion that he will submit to much painful restriction before he will desist, though in time he can, by improper punishment, be forced to do so.

By habit the dog's nose becomes his chief organ of sense. He relies on it implicitly. If his master returns after a short or long absence, though he may see him distinctly, he will circle around till he catches scent of him, thus verifying his eyesight, after which he is perfectly satisfied of correct identification.

If it should happen that the trainer so dominates the pupil, or that the latter is so subservient that he is disinclined to take any independent initiative, or that he is slow to engage in hunting, it is better to let him have a course of self-hunting under the trainer's supervision. That is to say, when working the puppy afield, the trainer permits him to seek in his own unhindered manner. The distinction between self-hunting, under the trainer's supervision, and independent self-hunting should be noted. Dogs thereby acquire great skill and confidence in the application of methods, developing their intelligence and knowledge to an astonishing degree.

The unrestrained pursuit of prey is the dog's greatest pleasure. Once he learns independent self-hunting, on opportunity he will steal away from home to indulge in it. He seeks the companionship of vagrant boys or dogs which are inclined to hunt like himself, which gives him the freedom from restraint which he so much values. When on an independent self-hunt the duration of his absence is sometimes measured by the degree of fatigue which he can suffer, at other times by the degree of hunger, or by the degree of hunger and fatigue combined. Sometimes he may be absent a few hours; sometimes several days, returning thereafter in a state of skin and bone, worn, weary and famished. When seeking thus for himself he will plod cheerfully through mud and snow; will swim cold streams of water; will work in brush and brier; will gallop bravely into woods and open, ever eager to find and capture, rarely desisting until physical exhaustion prevents him from engaging further in the pursuit. This may be beneficial to dogs of excessive timidity, but on the whole it is better to restrict the self-hunting to the limits set by the trainer.

However, the dog in one independent self-hunting outing learns more than he learns in weeks when under the domination of his trainer. Then all the natural hunting qualities and inclinations which are born in him have the free play unhindered. Self-hunting he learns to follow the trail with quickness, precision and enthusiasm; to distinguish the forward from the back trail; the body scent from the foot scent; the places which are likely to bc and which are not likely to be the haunts of birds ; and to mark the flight of flushed birds and its probable length. In short, he learns the values and relations of all the circumstances which are to be considered in the matter of pursuit and capture.

On the other hand, once that the dog has learned the delights and freedom of independent self-hunting there is no breaking him from indulging in it. He will sneak away whenever opportunity and inclination impel to it, prowling for miles everywhere throughout the surrounding country, generally in the company of some other dog or dogs of like proclivities. Confinement is the only preventive of such acts. However, this self-hunting proclivity may not in the least affect his zeal in working to the gun when opportunity offers.

The trainer should endeavor to afford ample opportunities to the pupil, and to this end an old, level-headed dog is a great assistant both as to finding the birds and as to example.

When the dog makes his points, the trainer seeks to prolong them as much as possible. He walks calmly up to the dog's side, strokes him gently along the back, and gently restrains him from breaking in. This is repeated time after time, gentleness and approval being exhibited when he does right and discreet disapproval when he does wrong.

If he is particularly obstinate or self-willed, a check cord, or a spike collar and check cord, may be used to advantage. The cord should have a light iron snap, such as is used on parts of harness, attached to one end of it. This enables the trainer to quickly snap it in the ring of the dog's collar without fuss or delay. With the check cord the dog can be easily kept under control when on point, so far as breaking in is under consideration.

The spike collar should be used with careful moderation. The average amateur does more harm in the use of it than he does good, although the same may be asserted equally of the whip or any other instrument of punishment. At all events, the use of it should be eschewed in all but the most obstinate, self-willed cases and in those cases if the trainer loses his temper when using it. A great deal of care is sometimes necessary to avoid such faults as blinking, trainer shyness, etc., when schooling the dog to stanchness on point.

In these early experiences the gun may be obstructive to the pupil's advancement. It may with advantage be kept in abeyance during the first lessons. It is not essential in teaching the pupil a proper degree of stanchness. He quickly learns its use, and when it is fired he has such an uncontrollable eagerness to secure possession of the bird that for a time he is lawless. On the other hand the average amateur is himself so over-eager to kill birds that the training of the dog is a remote matter when the opportunity to kill is presented, so that what should as much as possible be an orderly matter of schooling is then a disorganized scramble between man and dog.

However, as to the use of the gun, there are exceptional cases which will be benefited by it. Slothful, indolent dogs require the stimulus of successful capture, and there are others, again, which after working a time without material result, lose interest and cease effort. The trainer's own judgment.

When must be his guide under such circumstances. the dog is pointing or attempting to point he should be permitted to do so in his own natural manner. It is best to refrain from giving any caution or order till he either points or flushes. If the trainer is one out of a hundred he can do so, but if he is one of the other ninety-nine he must either bawl out orders or suffer untold anguish. Orders and multiplication of orders, however, no more assist a dog in learning to use his nose than they assist a man in guiding himself to find a needle by the sense of feeling in the dark less so, in fact, for the dog does not comprehend the meaning of many words.

After the dog flushes, the trainer may caution him or punish him according to the requirements of the case, as it was done intentionally or not, He then associates the displeasure with some definite event which, being painful, he seeks to avoid. Unintentional flushes should never be considered a cause for punishment, and this should hold good in respect to all other mistakes.

By permitting him to point or flush in his own way he learns what method results in error and what in success. Furthermore, left to his own judgment he learns to go to his birds without hesitation or apprehension of trouble, and points them at an intelligent estimate of distance, neither too far away from nor too close to them. In the case of timid dogs, actual encouragement may be necessary, and even willful flushes may need to be indulgently tolerated.

Unless a steady, well-trained dog can be used as a brace-mate for the green puppy, it is better to work him alone till he is fairly stanch. If the trainer can- not work one puppy according to rule, it requires no argument to demonstrate that he cannot work two or more.

The pointing of barnyard fowls by sight should be discouraged as much as possible. The education derived from it does not in the least assist the trainer when schooling the dog afield, The latter, when working to the gun, points, in the great majority of instances, by the sense of smell, and if he then seeks to point by sight, as he does when dallying with the barnyard fowls, he flushes oftener than he points. The functional powers of dogs' noses vary greatly. Of two dogs of equal intelligence, pace and stamina one may far excel the other in finding and pointing, and this due alone to the greater keenness of his nose. Many unintentional errors are made by dogs whose noses are dull. An intelligent dog, with such infirmity, will possibly develop into a useful performer, his superior knowledge enabling him to use his nose to the best advantage.

As to the length of time required to establish the point stanchly, nothing can be said definitely. It all depends on the pupil and the trainer's ability to per- mit him to learn. After a short schooling, some dogs of a gentle, deferential nature learn to point quickly in the interests of the gun, and even defer to a brace-mate, preferring the back to the point. Sometimes, when they observe their fellow reading, they play to take the back, thus anticipating the act of pointing. Others again play to get to the front at the earliest possible moment when a point is impending. However, as a general proposition, several weeks are required in which to properly school the dog to stanch point work, and sometimes this degree of proficiency is not reached till well into the second season, and in rare instances into the third. Occasionally the trainer will come across a dog which never can be taught to point reliably.

While the point when applied naturally is for the dog's individual advantage, by experience and the exercise of intelligence he learns to use it conjointly with the efforts of the shooter in the common purpose to capture. It is an amplification of the team work which he displays when working as a member of a pack or of a brace. He in time learns that the capture is affected by joint effort, even though such effort at first was a matter of disagreeable compulsion. After practical application has demonstrated the uses of schooling, he applies his efforts with great skill, and becomes original in manipulating the variable circumstances in a manner best calculated to serve the interests of the gun. To him a subordinate part is infinitely preferable to no part at all. This alone is sufficient to appeal to his self-interest, which is analogous to that of the little boy who beseeches the privilege of accompanying his big brother afield that he may carry the game which is killed.

The self-interest and consequently the efforts of the dog are easily maintained, if he is not excessively mistreated under a mistaken practice of training, or mistreated from a mistaken play of ill-temper.

The style of a point is considered a matter of first importance by some sportsmen, so much so that they assert that they would rather kill one bird over a magnificently spectacular point than many over a commonplace one. Nevertheless, there is a distinction between looking for pictures and looking for birds. A flashy hit-or-miss dog, with high-pressure legs, running across birds might make a point of incomparably greater beauty than that of a dog which worked out his points methodically and intelligently.

The dog with a high grade of bird sense rarely makes spectacular points. His work is of an all-day character, and he conducts it after the manner of an all-day workman. It is judgment and method as compared to snap work, the methodical professional against the enthusiastic amateur. Not that beautiful point work is objectionable, nor that good dogs now and then do not possess it, but it has not the exaggerated importance bestowed on it by the sportsman who values the spectacular manner over useful matter.

The first requisite of the setter and pointer is to find birds; the manner of it is incidental. Very few shooters who in the parlor declaim in ecstasy over the thrills and tremors of a sensational point live up to the ideal when in the field. Then a point is a point. If beautiful so much the better, if it is a true point; if false, so much the worse. At all events, when a shooter goes afield with a gun and dog it is safe to assume that the spectacular point is beautiful as an incident, though it is not the main purpose.

Some dogs from extreme caution learn to drop to point.

Others again, from getting lost on point, become weary of waiting, lie down to rest and learn it therefrom, while others, again, which have been taught to drop to shot, learn to drop in anticipation of the flush, which is gradually evolved into dropping to point.

CHAPTER IX

BACKING

BACKING, backsetting and backstanding denote the act of one dog standing more or less rigidly by sight to the point of another dog. The backing dog generally assumes much the same attitude when backing that he does when pointing, though in many instances the rigidity and intenseness therein are less. Not infrequently some backing dogs stand in a slack position, as they do naturally when there are no points at all to consider.

However enthusiastic and spirited may have been the backs at first, they in time, as the enthusiasm of youth and novelty pass away, generally become perfunctory. The dog learns that the purposes of the back, as enforced by the trainer, are repressive, that he is not to interfere with the pointing dog, and that therefore there is nothing of self-interest in it for himself. The backing act, which the dog displayed with a natural purpose, is nevertheless generally persisted in from education and habit.

As to its origin, backing is an act resulting from a process of reason, a perception of cause and effect, and is of use to the dog individually when a member of a pack. Some dogs take readily to backing as taught by man, others are induced with much difficulty to observe it, and, again, others cannot be induced to back at all. Much depends upon the intelligence and temperament of the individual as to whether he will back or not.

The natural act of backing has no reference what- ever to a man with a gun, who desires that his purposes with it shall not be obstructed.

It has been maintained, as against the theory and practice of intelligent backing, that the dog, first pointing the birds instinctively that a man might the better kill them thereby, also backed instinctively on occasion so that he would not interfere with the dog which was pointing, and thus would not jeopardize the success of the shooter. In support of this contention, the fact that the young puppies, when pointing sparrows and other small birds in the kennel yard and elsewhere, back each other, was adduced as proof positive of the instinctive origin of the act So much, by the old, and in most instances superficial, writers, was ascribed to instinct by way of explaining the dog's acts that one could justly wonder why the dog had brains at all ; or, having them, why he used them so little.

How this act which could be taught to but a relatively small number of the canine race, has to all the race become instinctive by inheritance, and how many other acts, taught to dogs generally, have not become likewise instinctive, is left by the old writers for the reader's own solution. However, if a writer does not understand certain phenomena of dog life, there is no easier way to dispose of it than to boldly assert that it is instinctive.

As to the pointing and backing of puppies, as above mentioned, the superficial observer failed to note that the point is followed by a chase of the little birds when flushed. The dogs have an instinctive impulse to pursue their prey, and in intelligent methods of successful pursuit they are astonishingly precocious.

Let us follow the first attempts of the puppies and observe thereby their rapid educational evolution.

They, seeing a sparrow on the ground hopping about,

sneak quickly toward it and then dash at full speed to seize it; it flies away and they give full chase, sometimes giving tongue merrily. Similar rash attempts result in failures. After a brief experience of this kind they quickly learn that the birds can fly, and that, in open pursuit of them, a capture is impossible. Then they observe greater precaution and therefrom approximate nearer to success. By sneaking craftily on the birds, the chances of getting within a better striking distance are many times increased, and by making play to the pointing dog the backing dog is in a strategic position to head the prey off or turn it to the pointing dog. Thus the back is simply a part of the team work in the attempt to capture.

Team work, of which backing is a part, is one of the first things learned by all breeds of dogs which have an opportunity to hunt in company. It is analogous to the running cunning of the greyhound. Two puppies, intent on capturing a barnyard fowl, show this unmistakably. One draws up and points; the other backs. The alarmed fowl walks away; the pointing puppy draws forward; the backing puppy whips stealthily around to head off the fowl, and then they have it between them in a hazardous position. Left to themselves in their attack upon it, they display pretty team work, so far as intelligent management and effort are concerned.

This also is frequently the manner employed to capture a rabbit or other animal which is lying concealed from view, and whose whereabouts is known only by the sense of smell.

In drawing on the little birds by sight, the puppy employs much the same strategic efforts that, in his more mature years and more serious efforts, he employs in drawing on game birds by the use of his nose. The efforts by sight are applied in the first crude attempts; the efforts by nose are applied in the skilful manner which comes from experience and knowledge, though both come from the instinctive impulse to seek game animals for food.

In the pursuit of fur the setter and pointer draw on it in much the same manner that they do on birds, but with less caution. For instance, if a rabbit is jumped they pursue it hotly, giving tongue eagerly the while. On birds they are silent, as they need must be if they are to achieve success. There are exceptions to this, rare, however; some setters and pointers whimper and give tongue on a trail much after the manner of a rabbit dog.

Let us now consider the dog more specifically as a member of a pack and also consider the intelligent team work which such membership imposes. He much prefers to work with one of his own kind. The joint efforts of a number are far more certain to result in success than are the efforts of the lone individual. Therefore, whether wild or domestic, they much prefer to hunt with each other.

Wolves take distinct parts in the struggle to effect a capture. One or two may make a sham attack on a cow while others seize and kill her momentarily unguarded calf. Coyotes have been known to stalk themselves with excellent judgment in such manner and places that, as one or more of their number pursued the fleeing antelope, it passed by the others in turn, and each in turn took up the pursuit and relieved the pursuer, so that the antelope was pitted against a relay of wolves.

The greyhound, when pursuing animals as swift or swifter than itself, invariably learns to run cunning if he is permitted to have even a moderate continuous experience.

In running cunning, when two or more are pursuing together, one dashes forward at full speed to press the fleeing jack rabbit, antelope, etc., while his fellow is running less swiftly behind. The purpose of the leading hound is to press the prey to a turn from its course. If he succeeds, instantly his fellow dashes forward at top speed across the angle thus formed, heading the prey off if possible, and in any event getting closer up to it. He then takes up the running, while his fellow behind watches alertly for the next turn, and when it comes he cuts across the corner. Sometimes the hindmost dog, without losing speed, will rear high up so that he may see over the leading dog, and thereby note what the prey is doing.

Every time that a turn is made the prey runs on two sides of a triangle, while the hindmost dog runs on but one. This is a sufficient advantage in favor of the dogs to insure their final success. After the hindmost dog can cut in ahead of their prey, there then is a dog in front and one in the rear of it, and it is in a perilous situation. The backing dog may be said to be backing cunning, for it is analogous in its purposes to the running cunning of the greyhound. Either act is but one of many similar ones.

The country dog, be he cur or otherwise, has some neighboring dog with which he is on friendly terms, and which he seeks as company for his prowling expeditions through the woods and fields. In time the self-hunters learn all the strategy essential to success. If they approach a brush pile which gives good promise of a rabbit, do they go up to it together? That is not their procedure after they be- come educated. One advances to the pile to start the rabbit, while the other, in manner similar to that of the backing dog, takes a strategic position to seize it when it springs from cover, or failing to do so, that he may turn it to his fellow with a good chance of capture.

All the acts of dogs when hunting together have a direct bearing to the common purpose, as it refers directly to their own interests that is to say, the capture. Their knowledge and skill thus come from intelligence and experience. That the acts are sometimes learned very quickly proves none the less that they are so derived. In no other manner could they be acquired.

Backing has a direct reference to the capture of the prey, and is conclusively proven by the well-known fact that an intelligent dog, even when most thoroughly trained, will refuse to back a dog which, within his observation, false points a few times. He observes that the false-pointing dog is unreliable, and that as there is nothing to the point to be pursued or captured, so there is no use in preparing to seize or pursue. This also denotes that the act refers to himself, and not a man with a gun. In practical field work the only material advantage of backing is that it prevents interference with the pointing dog, although it has the sentimental value of being pleasing to the eye as a spectacular act.

In such instances as a man shoots alone and owns but one dog, it is not of the slightest importance whether his dog will point or not. But when dogs are hunted together, it is of importance that they be made steady to back; or, if they will not back, then that they be taught to drop promptly to order

A dog which, refusing to break, either presses ahead to steal the point or flush the birds, will thoroughly spoil more sport than all other causes combined. Some dogs, otherwise good, behave very badly when working with a dog which refuses to back. Under such conditions they misbehave generally. They will not submit to their points being stolen; they, rather than tolerate interference, will wilfully go ahead and flush to prevent any points being made at all, or perform so resentfully and jealously that the standard of the work is ragged and poor. Therefore, when a dog is pointing no other dog should be permitted to interfere with him.

Backing well and stanchly, while not indispensable, is an accomplishment which puts a needed and useful finish to the work of dogs when in company afield with their fellows, and besides being pleasing to the eye, it adds to the pleasure and ease of the shooter in handling them, and thus to the success of the gun.

Until the dog has learned the purposes of pointing, he shows no inclination to back. Thus puppies which are raised alone have no knowledge of what the act of pointing means, though they very quickly learn it on proper opportunity.

In teaching the puppy stanchness to the back, it is best to have an old, reliable dog to do the pointing. The point being made, the puppy's attention is attracted to it, with as little noise and fuss as possible. With an exaggerated caution of movement and manner, the trainer endeavors to impress on him the gravity and importance of the event. After he ob- serves that birds are to the point, he will acquire an enthusiastic interest in it on his own account.

Commonly the puppy's first efforts will be spirited

attempts to flush. They are the natural acts of ignorant puppies. After a few or many lessons, when the pointing dog engages the interest of the puppy, and the latter is well in hand, the trainer walks forward to flush. If the puppy attempts to follow, he is taken back to the spot whence he started and cautioned. The trainer acts slowly, gravely, patiently and quietly if he acts aright. The portentous manner will not fail to impress the puppy as he notes it in conjunction with the point.

Dogs are exceedingly imitative. This the trainer may readily observe by assuming a crouchy, stealthy manner in an open field, as if he were stalking some prey. The dog will likely imitate his actions. How- ever, it is not wise in this manner to deceive a dog, as it tends to impair his confidence in the deceiver.

Whenever the puppy attempts to press forward when on back he must be cautioned or be taken to the place whence he started. This impresses on him that he is not to go forward when his fellow is pointing. The cord and peg may be applied usefully to keep him in place if he is difficult to manage.

After the birds are flushed and a kill is made, the puppy will gain a comprehension of the purposes of the acts. Some puppies learn to back quickly ; with others it may be necessary to repeat the lessons through many days or weeks.

Even after weeks of teaching, a puppy may seem to have no interest in backing, yet some day when he comes suddenly and unexpectedly on his brace-mate pointing, he may astonish and gratify his trainer by backing instantaneously and well. The trainer may devise ways to run him on sight of the pointing dog when he does not suspect a point, arranging, however, to be in a position to interpose if he attempts to steal the point or to flush.

Pointers as a rule are much more easily taught .to point and back than are setters. Some dogs are so deferential that they will play to take the backing position the moment that they see their fellow making game, while others will steal the point on opportunity, or back and draw alternately till the point is stolen or the birds are flushed.

It is a branch of training in which the trainer must use infinite tact and patience. Nothing is gained by hurry. Punishment will deter the pupil from running in on a pointing dog, and to that extent it is of value, but it does not teach him how to back. It may, however, teach him to blink.

By persistent attempts to enforce the act of backing there will be but few cases which will result in failure. On the other hand, half-hearted and fitful attempts will result in many failures. Persistency, common sense, patience and tact in applying methods and affording opportunities are essential factors in this branch as they are in all others.

CHAPTER X

ROADING AND DRAWING

R OADING and drawing are terms used to denote the act of the dog in locating the birds, by the functional powers of the nose which he possesses.

Roading more specifically applies to following the foot cent ; drawing to following the body scent. Colloquially speaking, the effort of the dog to determine the whereabouts of the birds, after he has struck their trail or caught the scent of them, is called "locating."

Generally, aside from the individual differences of manner which all dogs exhibit, one compared with another, setters and pointers follow birds in two ways ; namely, by the foot scent or the body scent. When following by foot scent the dog devotes his attention to following the course of the birds in all its windings, using his nose to distinguish the scent which hovers around the tracks, as the handler, in an analogous manner, might use his eyes to distinguish and follow them.

In following the foot scent, dogs vary in skill from that of the potterer which puzzles about, following the back or forward track with equal stupidity and inefficiency, to that of the dog which roads with methodical celerity and accuracy.

A reasonable degree of quickness is essential to fair performance. The longer and further the birds run ahead of .the roading dog, the greater likelihood is there of complications which may result in the loss of the trail, or their secure refuge in dense cover, or their escape by wing. Dogs which follow by the foot scent carry a lower nose, as a rule, than do those which follow by the body scent.

The dog which locates by body scent is guided by the particles of scent floating in the air, though his nose may be only at such height as he naturally carries it. When he catches a scent, however faint, he darts quickly to and fro, following it up quickly till it becomes strong enough to follow direct to the birds. It is analogous to the manner which a man might be supposed to adopt if he caught scent of roses in the field and followed the clue up to the rose bushes from which the fragrance emanated.

A dog whose nose is keen and whose brain is sound will locate his birds with astonishing quickness by the body scent, but there are different grades of performers in this method, as there are also in the one aforementioned.

Whichever style of "locating" is used by the dog, to be a successful finder of birds it is necessary that he be able to determine the forward track from the backward track, and to locate the hiding place of the birds with a reasonable degree of quickness. The accomplishment of pointing stanchly is of but little utility if the dog cannot find the birds to point.

Whether they locate by foot scent or body scent, clogs vary greatly when compared with each other in respect to proficiency in locating. To strike scent some trust to their speed and the consequent wide area which they beat out, pointing the birds well when they happen to run across them. Such dogs may have distinctly inferior ability in following a scent, and yet, by pointing with much firmness and spirit when squarely on the birds, they may create a much better impression than a less pretentious but more meritorious performer. Wide range, high speed, and spirited points are not necessarily indicative of good finding and locating ability. There are many sham "high-class" performers.

Whether ranging fast or slow, the dog should have his mind concentrated on the use of his nose, as well as on beating out the ground with good judgment. When ranging in this manner he will pick up light scents and follow them to a successful find ; will detect the scent of a trail which he is running squarely across, and will have in mind the leeward side of all places as the best route to follow, thus "having the wind" of the birds from the covers in which they lie hidden. In the results, there are all the differences between those of intelligent, finished effort, and those of chance effort applied hit or miss. Brains are quite as essential to the successful use of the nose as they are in any other line of effort. A dog with keen powers of scent and a dull brain may show fragments of brilliant work betimes when the circumstances happen to combine favorably, but as a whole his work is irregular, ragged and unsatisfactory.

On the other hand, a dog with a good brain and a dull nose may do quite satisfactory work.

Why two dogs, highly intelligent and possessing good noses, the one following by foot scent, the other by body scent, should vary so much in their respective methods of locating is not known. Men, however, vary quite as much in the methods employed in shooting, some aiming the gun, others snap shooting by a sense of direction, others again shooting without much aiming or sense of direction, trusting largely to a beneficent providence or the law of chances for material results.

Whichever method the dog adopts naturally in locating is his best method. Locating by following the foot scent is inferior to locating by following the body scent, but the trainer is powerless in respect to enforcing the better method if the dog chooses to adopt the other. However, he can do much to mar it by ill-timed interference or persistent meddlesome-ness.

The habit of perpetually cautioning and checking the dog, to make him go slow when he is reading or locating birds, a fault displayed by most amateur trainers, should be avoided. The effort, on the contrary, should be directed toward encouraging the dog to locate as quickly as possible, consistently with his ability to do so truly and properly. In this relation, the trainer would do well to bear in mind that there is an important distinction between quickness and hurry.

Some dogs have the ability to locate either by following the foot scent or the body scent, conducting themselves according to the conditions governing at the time in the interest of the best success. Dogs of inferior range, yet skillful in locating and with good judgment in planning their work besides having the power to concentrate their minds on it, not infrequently distinguish themselves as excellent field performers.

The trainer should not tolerate any pottering work when a dog is puzzling on the foot scent. Drive him from the pottering with the whip. The dog which habitually sniffs at a single track one after another, returning to the same tracks time after time to sniff them again, as if he liked them for their own sake, thus leaving the trail to get cold and lost, is worthless.

To be of any value in locating he must road a little faster than the birds run, otherwise they will run clear away from him. On the other hand, when the dog is picking out the trail and is actually going ahead on it, it is better then to leave the matter entirely to him. No theory of the trainer as to where the birds have rim should be opposed to the doings of the dog wheri he is reading. Even if the trainer actually knows where the birds are, he should permit the dog to find them in his own way.

If the trainer is seeking to secure a shot as a matter of first consideration, the schooling of the dog then is necessarily secondary to it. The pupil must learn to locate by his own experience, and the trainer can do but little more than to present to him the opportunities to exercise his powers in that respect.

A simple illustration will enable the novice to better understand the distinction between foot scent and body scent. Let it be assumed that on a dry plain a small body of sheep have passed by. He desires to follow them, but they are out of sight. He notes that their tracks, which are quite plain in a few places, indistinct or entirely lost in others, are followed with more or less difficulty, according to their continuity or their faintness or clearness of imprints.

However, it is noted that there is a perceptible line of dust along and over the trail. It is quite visible to the eye. By following it at high speed by sight before it is dissipated by the breeze, the flock may be accurately followed and overtaken. The particles of dust visible to the eye in this case correspond to the particles of body scent which the dog follows by the sense of smell, and the tracks are analogous in a way to the trail left by the birds.

The best of dogs will occasionally make mistakes, and this may be truthfully said of the best of men also. Mistakes made when the dog is endeavoring to do his best should always be silently overlooked.

The puzzle peg, a device intended to be tied on the dog's under jaw, in such a position that it projects some three or four inches forward on it, was anciently devised to make him carry a high nose and thus force him to follow the birds by their body scent. It is a useless and cruel instrument in practice hence description of it is unnecessary. All mechanical means are useless unless when applied to correct in the nose a cause which exists in the brain.

It is better to permit and encourage the dog to seek in his best manner as his nature impels or permits.

CHAPTER XL

RANGING

To THE novice the manner in which a dog seeks his prey is a matter of but little consideration, for, if the latter gallops out in search of birds, or even gallops at all, if he will but continue galloping it would seem that nothing more were necessary or requisite. It, however, is far from being such a simple matter.

In practice the novice will sooner or later find that a dog, though he be of great range and speed, may have distinctly inferior finding abilities. Good heels require good brains and noses to direct them.

The best ranger is the dog which "stays out at his work," beating out the likely ground in front and on both sides of the general course, and all this with such method and regularity as the nature of the ground best permits. His judgment should be so good that he forecasts the course of the shooter in a general way, or determines it by wise observation, and keeps it ever as a base of operations from which to work.

Let us assume that the dog is seeking quail. Bare or unpromising country, such as plowed ground, closely grazed pasture, etc., he skirts or entirely avoids. He notes such covers to the right and left as are likely to afford a habitat for the birds, and he ranges from one of them to the other, observing due economy in following his course so that he will cover the most ground with the least galloping consistent with the work to be done. He goes through cover when in his wise judgment it is necessary to do so to insure the best chances of success; or, taking the wind to the best advantage, he gallops along other stretches of cover which are likely to be used by the birds as a place of refuge. Sometimes he skirts around an entire field to hit off the trail of moving birds, while at other times he goes through it, accordingly as the wind, scenting conditions, etc., dictate. From experience he learns the kinds of ground which the birds most frequent, and the times of day in which they are most likely to be found in them.

When the birds are plentiful he beats out a much smaller area of ground than when they are scarce.

In the broad prairie, the chicken country where to the untrained eye there is little difference of ground surface apparent, the dog may not need to exercise so much good judgment as in seeking quail, but he needs to exercise it, nevertheless. The prairie, from where the beholder stands to the horizon, has its lesser and greater undulations, with their innumerable miniature water sheds, forming networks of hollows, in which are much coarser and ranker grasses than are those of the higher ground. Therein are concealment and shelter to the chickens during the night and the midday hours.

In the morning and evening, their favorite time of food-seeking, the chickens frequent the grain fields in the season when the grain is fit for their food; or the higher ground, where the growth is shorter, when insect life is more abundant.

Of the dogs which range at high speed, a large percentage run faster than their noses and judgment warrant if we consider the best possible results. Indeed, some run so fast and hurriedly that they do not take time to dwell even for a moment in searching out the likely "places, although they have the general appearance of earnest and good industry. They simply are high-class pretenders. There is a distinction between a dog running merrily, as he would in a park, and a dog ranging properly in search of game.

A dog may be so intent in the use of his eyes to pick out the easiest going that he gives no attention to the practical use of his nose. In a country known to contain birds he may work over great areas without finding other than the birds which he happens to run directly across. He on the other hand may have the speed and good finding intention which are shown by continuous industry and judgment, and yet, from functional dullness of the nose as an organ of scent, be incapacitated as a finder. Before a dog can range in the best manner he must have had sufficient experience to learn what sections of ground and cover the birds prefer for a habitat and a food supply; what are their general habits of life, and what peculiar devices they exercise to evade pursuit. In a manner it is much the same knowledge that a shooter himself should possess.

Of two shooters, the one knowing at a glance what section of certain grounds the birds seek for food and shelter, the other ignorant or heedless of their habitat, habits, and the manner of working the ground to the best advantage, no explanation is needed as to which would be the most successful.

The intelligence and industry which the shooter must exercise in bringing success to the use of the gun are not unlike those which the dog must exercise similarly in bringing success to the use of his nose.

As to working out the ground properly there is no

arbitrary method. What might be a thorough working of it by one dog might not be so at all when done similarly by some other dog. The one might have a very keen nose, which would command a wide scope, and therewith might take every intelligent advantage of wind and ground, the other, owing to a dull nose and its consequent smaller scope, might be unable to work out the ground properly if he followed the same lines set by his keener-nosed rival.

Local conditions also have their importance. In a close country the range should not be so far that the dog is out of sight for appreciable lengths of time, for then the shooter cannot know what the dog is doing. If he then gets on a point he is difficult to find, and if he flushes and chases, the shooter is ignorant of it. If he points a mile away on a prairie it is more of labor than of pleasure to go so far to him for a shot.

The matter of pace is essential to consider in connection with ranging, and with it also the matter of endurance. As hinted herein, a very fast dog, ex- tended to his utmost in speed, is rarely a thorough hunter. Being over-extended, he has not the time to consider or search out the nooks and corners with the care and thoroughness necessary to the best finding results, nor time to concentrate his mind on anything other than mere running. On the other hand, a dog may show good speed for a while, then slow down to a trot, working a while and loafing a while.

The best pace is a steady, swinging gallop, which is easily within the dog's physical compass, and such as he can maintain all day long. If to this he adds bird sense and concentrates his powers on his work, remaining out at it constantly, he as a success is in pleasing contrast to the

116

flashy, over-speeded dog whose mind is concentrated solely on picking out a clear course to run in. Too much speed often denotes an ignorance of hunting rather than knowledge of it, as it relates to the service of the gun.

Aside from the matter of pace, the most common examples of bad ranging are as follows: When a dog takes his casts, be they long or short, straight out in any direction in which he first starts, generally up or across wind, then turns and comes directly back to his handler on nearly the same line which marked his course in going out. On the return, in most instances, he forgets that he has a nose while using his eye to watch his handler as he hurries straight to him. In any event, it is not then necessary that he should use his nose on ground which he a moment before ran over.

A particularly annoying phase of this style of ranging is the taking of a straight line directly ahead in the course of the shooter. Thus most of the time the shooter and the dog are following the same line. More than half of such a dog's time and effort is wasted, for it takes him as long to return as it does to go out. He necessarily is a poor finder. He knows no difference between the best and the worst ground. He may point birds when he happens to run across them, as he is sure to do sooner or later in a bird country, for even the shooter will himself walk up birds every now and then ; but so far as any real merit is concerned such a dog- has none,

Another faulty manner of ranging is when the dog turns to the rear at the end of a cast and swings in behind his handler or on to ground which he covered before in his previous cast, thus repeatedly and uselessly crossing his course. Some dogs acquire the habit of working entirely

117

on one side of the handler's course. If forced to cast on the opposite side, they are intent on returning to their favorite position, and soon craftily return to it. Others have the extremely objectionable fault of working behind their handlers. Still others work very close for a while, regardless of the character of the ground, then take an extremely long cast with little judgment or purpose to it, returning after a time and resuming the pottering range.

The wind and its direction are important factors in ranging; all dogs work best when the shooter is walking against it. They can then beat across it to and fro, turning up wind at the end of their casts if they turn properly, thus having the best advantages of catching scent of the birds which are within range of their noses.

If the shooter is going down wind the dog, though he can beat across wind as before, must necessarily turn down wind at the end of his casts if he keeps best in place relatively to the shooter. If the dog turns up wind under these circumstances, he turns on to ground which he has worked, making loops at the end of his casts, all of which results in inferior effort.

In their ability to work out the ground regardless of whether the shooter walks up, down or across wind, dogs vary greatly in their powers. Some dogs, good rangers up wind, seem to lose all ideas of intelligent ranging when the shooter walks down wind; others perform well regardless of the course of the shooter.

When the shooter walks straight across wind he gives the dog the most difficult proposition to range to, since if he then casts straight across the shooter, he must go straight up and down wind. The wise dog, of good sense and good experience, works well regardless of his handler's course, for he casts out and stays out far enough to have a free fling according to the circumstances.

It is better to give the dog experience in working out the ground regardless of the wind, for many times it happens in a day's shooting that, owing to the nature of the grounds and general course of the hunt, an up wind course cannot be followed.

Quartering denotes that the dog crosses to and fro in front of the shooter on lines as parallel and equi- distant as may be. It is an artificial method, and no doubt is of use in a section where the ground is favor- able to it and where birds are likely to frequent all parts of the ground indiscriminately. The English authorities emphasize its importance. In America, where the grounds exhibit all kinds of irregularities as to surface and covers, it is much better that the dog should beat out the ground intelligently from one likely point to another. The habitats of the birds are so irregularly placed, and there is so much barren ground mixed in with that which is fertile, that a set form of quartering is neither taught nor desired by the majority of shooters.

In quartering, the dog covers as much ground as his nose and speed will permit consistently with the size of the field or ground to be worked, and at the same time with keeping in front of the shooter. It is apparent that if the dog makes his casts too wide he will not be able to cut out his parallels and at the same time keep in front of the shooter. In sections where on the one hand the intelligent' ranger succeeds in rinding birds in abundance, they on the other might appear to be very scarce when sought by a dog which hunted parallel lines across his handler's course.

A dog which does not range well naturally is capable of but little improvement from the efforts of his handler. If he comes in repeatedly as a habit, a crack or a cut of the whip, as he comes in, will tend to keep him from coming entirely in; but instead of going out to work when so unpleasantly received he may sulk. At all events, his imperfect judgment is not to be materially mended by any efforts of his handler. Constant whistling and signaling and directing may help the faulty dog to a limited extent, but the handler then is furnishing all the brains and doing the thinking for the dog which the latter, if of the right grade as a worker, would think for himself.

To teach the dog quartering, implicit obedience to the whistle and signals of the hand must be taught as a pre-requisite. The course is always up wind. Then, when the dog is ranging, the handler walks to and fro from left to right, keeping him on the correct parallels across wind as near as he can, and turning him when at the proper distance at the end of them. This is continued day after day till the dog-will, from mere habit, follow the artificial range thus established. It requires a world of labor and patience to each it thoroughly. After it is taught it has certain spectacular features which appeal to the novice, but which to the expert suggest a worthless redundancy of effort.

The theory of brace work when the dogs quarter their ground is that they work on wider parallels in their casts, which alternate so that neither works on the other's ground except when turning at the end of their casts. They should cross in front of their handler at about the same time, should cast about the same distance to the right and left, and should make their turns at the ends of their casts at about the same moment. To approximate, even remotely, to this degree of refinement, the dog must work independently, must be nearly equal in pace and industry, and in general must have the same ideas of quartering; in short, they must be fairly well matched.

Dogs develop idiosyncrasies in quartering as they do in free ranging. One may cast well on one side, turning up wind properly, while at the end of his cast on the other side he turns downwind; or he may cast irregularly wide and close, or wide on one side and short on the other, or come to his handler in the middle of his cast, or cast to the rear of his handler betimes, etc., or be working outside the boundaries which are most advantageous to the shooter's success. A point made a half mile or more away imposes a great loss of time and extra walking or riding on the shooter, as do also the long searches for the dog when he is lost on point, and the latter is a frequent occurrence when the dog works beyond bounds. The dog which so works is a semi-self-hunter, and is a very laborious dog to handle.

CHAPTER XII

DROPPING TO SHOT AND WING.

DROPPING to shot and wing are terms which denote that, at the rise of the bird or birds, or the report of the gun, the dog drops instantly to the ground. It is much more ornamental than useful, and besides has some distinct disadvantages.

There are many sportsmen who set an exaggerated value on what may be termed the embellishments of training, such as quartering, dropping to shot and wing, toho, etc., and who profess to take more pleasure from the manner in which the dog performs than in the material results of his efforts.

The main purpose of the dog's service, however, is one of utility; the embellishments, though desirable, hold a secondary place. If, therefore, the dog is a good and useful servant, and yet possessed of little style, he is far superior to a stylish nonentity.

While it is a matter of constant recurrence that the shooter finds it necessary to order the dog to lie down on certain occasions in the hunting field or at home, to prevent his interference, to stop his prowling, or to make him cease hunting, yet it is not desirable that he be made to drop in a machine-like manner when there is no real occasion for it. The contention that it puts a more artistic finish to the dog's work, and that it is a deterrent to breaking shot, chasing and breaking in, is a matter of pure fancy. It comes under the head of a
trick performance, much as if the dog were to turn a somersault at the report of the gun, and is almost as

irrelevant.

There is nothing in the rise of the bird or the report of the gun that can be usefully supplemented by the drop of the dog, nor is the act of special importance as a preventive of shot breaking, breaking in, or chasing.

If the dog is unsteady, he does not drop to wing in practice, whatever he may do in theory.

The enforcement of steadiness to shot and wing is one of the easiest parts of the dog's training to compass, and it is infinitely much easier to teach than it is to teach the dog to drop to shot or wing.

The disadvantages encountered in teaching it and after it is taught, are that, some punishment being necessary in its enforcement, there is danger that the dog unwittingly may be taught to blink or to be gun-shy, or both. The punishment, being directly associated with the report of the gun and the rise of the bird, at a juncture when the mind of the dog is intensely concentrated on the birds and his every desire "red in their capture, is by him likely to be entered erroneously. He may consider that he has won the disapproval of his master, and has been punished for meddling with the birds at all. After a few ; a.niui experiences he is quite likely to consider the rt as a signal for punishment for some cause of which he is entirely ignorant, or for no cause at all.

In cold, rainy weather, when the ground is muddy or saturated with cold water, or when there are ice and snow, no sportsman who has a right heart would force his dog to lie down merely to gratify a fancy.

In briers and thorns it is often painful for the dog to drop.

Sometimes, if the dog trained to drop to wing flushes in over, or at a distance from the shooter where he is out of sight, he will lie a long time in the dropped position waiting for the order to go on.

Not infrequently it happens that the dog, after a time of rigid schooling to dropping to wing, anticipates the rise of the bird from every noise which he happens to hear, or from the act of the shooter in walking up to flush, and therefore drops before the bird takes wing. By degrees he becomes more deferential, and anticipates by dropping safely before the bird rises at all, and in time this degenerates into dropping on point, a most undesirable manner of pointing.

Dropping to point adds greatly to the difficulties of the shooter in reference to the dog, for the latter must then be watched unceasingly. If he happens to drop when the shooter does not see him, a long search to find him may thereby be entailed, and indeed he may not be found on point at all, it being necessary to whistle or call him from it. A little cover suffices to conceal a dog when lying down.

When dropped to shot, it is impossible for a dog, lying down, to mark the flight of live birds or the whereabouts of dead birds with the precision that he can attain when standing up. The marking of birds is an accomplishment which all dogs do not possess, it is true, but nevertheless it is a most useful accomplishment, and much to be desired.

Dropping to shot, if taught, should be made a part of the

yard training. It is taught in precisely the same manner that the oral command and signal are taught.

The manner of teaching the dog to drop to shot and wing must be governed much by his disposition. If he is exceedingly timid, intelligent care and deliberation should be exercised. In any event, he should be taught to drop promptly and cheerfully to order, apart from any considerations of dropping to wing or shot. The yard training in this respect should be especially thorough when the trainer contemplates making it a part of the work on game.

In teaching the dog to drop to command, with the aid of the whip, the trainer should observe the greatest care to hit the dog in the same place each time, as on the shoulder. When he feels his shoulder thus hit, he will drop instantly without any oral command after he is schooled properly. Indeed, after a time he will drop when his shoulder is merely touched. It in its way is recognized as an imperative command, for the threat of the whip closely supplements it.

Heavy charges of powder are unnecessary in the lessons. An old pistol using percussion caps is quite sufficient. As to the manner of using it, the trainer, with a check cord five or six feet long, leads the dog about, snaps a cap at a favorable juncture, taps the dog on the shoulder as aforementioned, and enforces obedience to the report in the same manner as if it were an oral order. This is repeated, lesson after lesson, till the dog will drop promptly to the report.

The lesson should be given kindly and pleasantly. It can be conducted without filling the dog with terror and the consequent desire to escape, or fear of the gun. Common sense on the part of the teacher is essential to determine how the lessons should be conducted. Under no circumstances should he attempt this part of the dog's education if the least degree of gun-shyness is exhibited, nor is it wise to attempt enforcing it in the field if the pupil has any faults which require punishment to correct them.

Dropping to wing and all attempts to teach it should be kept in abeyance till the latter part of the dog's field education; in the early part there are complications enough without importing any unnecessary extra ones.

It is taught at first by ordering the dog to drop every time that a bird is flushed within his sight or hearing, whether he pointed it or not. The trainer endeavors also to take advantage of every opportunity which presents itself in the furtherance of his purpose, such as, for instance, walking up beside the dog when he is on point, flushing the bird then, and at the same time, if necessary, giving him a cut on the shoulder with the whip, as when teaching him to drop in the yard lessons.

The trainer, however, should avoid the extreme of making himself too much of a factor in the rise of the bird, else the dog will drop when he is approached, in anticipation of being forced to drop a moment or two later. By many impressive repetitions of the act in conjunction with the rise of the bird, the dog in time comes to recognize the first sound of wings as an order to drop.

Patience and careful progress should be observed in giving these lessons. If there is too much hurry or violence, it is quite an easy matter to injure the dog's work in other respects.

When a dog is over-fatigued it is not wise to enforce dropping to shot or wing too strictly. He may find it such a comfortable position that it is to his liking. When greatly fatigued, dogs, when standing on point for a long while, learn to drop on their own initiative, and from this as a beginning they may learn to drop on their points habitually. Once acquired, there is no way of remedying the fault.

CHAPTER XIII

BREAKING SHOT, BREAKING IN, CHASING

THE different manifestations of unsteadiness are termed breaking shot, breaking in, and chasing, and all have their origin in the desire of the dog to capture the bird. It is all quite in keeping with his nature and natural manner of acquiring possession of his prey.

Breaking shot is when the dog breaks away at the report of the gun.

Breaking in denotes that the dog, as the term signifies, breaks in and flushes the birds, either before or after making a point, and chasing signifies according to its common meaning.

The amateur, whose pre judgments are based on his own purposes as being the true data for estimating the dog's duties, is prone to consider the different forms of unsteadiness as manifestations of perversity or malicious harmfulness. From the dog's standpoint, however, the handler has no more relation to the pursuit of game than he would have to a bone which the dog might be gnawing.

While the dog takes a certain degree of pleasure in the pursuit of game, a material purpose, the capture of the prey, dominates, and thus his eager pursuit has a basis of self-interest. The latter must be preserved therefore it is seldom good training to attempt to check his unsteadiness too suddenly. It is better done by easy degrees, even if the dog is distinctly hard-headed in his obstinacy.

Steadiness is one of the easiest parts of the training to enforce when the trainer engages in it seriously, although it is one of the most difficult for the average shooter, on account of his failure to methodically control the dog by mechanical means.

Some nice judgment should be exercised as to how much freedom to give the dog, in case of timidity, apathetic interest, natural indolence, etc. Some dogs, whose self-interest is exceptionally assertive, will hunt with the greatest enthusiasm for themselves, while hunting only with half-heartedness for their masters. Thus the matter of how much restraint should be exercised is one of expediency, which must be determined by the good judgment of the trainer.

While giving the puppy's unsteadiness serious consideration, the amateur should avoid any exhibitions of it himself. If he breaks shot to capture a wounded bird, or manifests undue haste and excitement when in the vicinity of birds, it is unreasonable to expect steadiness under such circumstances on the part of the puppy, or indeed on the part of a thoroughly trained dog. The enormity of the offense as manifested by the puppy consists not so much in the act itself as in spoiling a shot for the trainer. Many amateur trainers are more intent on the pleasures of the sport than on the advancement of the dog's schooling, therefore the error is in the nature of a personal interference with their purpose.

Chasing rabbits should be corrected first. Viewed from a schooling standpoint, the act may be a fault or not, accordingly as the dog may or may not need an incentive to effort. Timid dogs gain self-confidence and boldness, while lazy dogs acquire more industry and enthusiasm from indulging in it.

When the trainer attempts to teach the dog to forbear chasing, the procedure then is to make the act painful instead of pleasurable. The trainer by punishment proceeds to establish in the dog's mind an association of unpleasant ideas in reference to the rabbit. This is quickly done by shooting a rabbit ahead of the dog, on favorable opportunity, of which many present themselves when a dog is addicted to the habit of chasing. The dog will manifest the greatest elation when the rabbit is shot. However, the trainer fastens a check cord to the dog's collar, and with the rabbit and whip in the left hand administers a good whipping to him. At intervals, the rabbit is thrust in his face, the trainer at the same time exclaiming Hi ! Hi ! Hi ! with some cuts of the whip sandwiched in. The dog credits all the hurts to the rabbit, and learns to associate it with pain accordingly.

It is commonly held to be bad training to shoot a rabbit ahead of a dog. It is so if one indulges in it with a thoroughly trained dog as a matter of filling the game bag. Discrimination between what encourages a dog to chase and what deters him from chasing should be considered. Shooting a rabbit ahead of a chasing dog and punishing him for it bring the act and the object in direct and painful association. After a time, if the dog at the first view of a fleeing rabbit, forgets himself on the impulse of the moment, and starts to chase, the warning cry Hi Hi! Hi! will check him, and on second thought he will desist. The punishment must be persisted in until the dog ignores the rabbit temptation reliably.

The correction for unsteadiness to shot and wing is also administered ,on the theory of associating the errors with pain, but in practice much more care needs to be exercised than in breaking the dog of rabbit chasing. By injudicious punishment, it is quite as easy to teach the dog to forbear hunting birds at all as it is to forbear chasing rabbits. There is a degree of punishment which will deter the dog from chasing and breaking in ; there is a further degree which will deter him from hunting at all, and there is still a further degree which will cause him to blink. He should never be punished so severely or so persistently that he shows hesitation or loss of confidence in himself or handler. It is much better to make haste slowly, accomplishing advancement safely.

Dogs of a sensitive, deferential disposition may be steadied at the warning cry, Hi ! Hi ! Hi ! and words of disapproval alone. On a dog of a bolder nature, resolutely intent on chasing, the check cord is put while he is pointing, and when the birds rise he is per- mitted to dash forward fifteen or twenty feet before being snubbed and brought back to the place whence he started.

An aged, experienced dog, which has become a confirmed shot breaker may be dealt with still more severely. A spike collar is effective in making a prompt cure. Place it upon his neck when he is working. Tie the choke with a piece of twine, so that it will not slip backward and forward as a choke collar, thus resting on his neck in manner similar to his ordinary kennel collar. When he points, the trainer walks up to him quietly, fastens the check cord into his collar, adjusts it so it will uncoil freely, then shoots and permits the dog to run into the collar when he breaks shot. The impetus of the dog breaks the twine, and the collar then hugs his neck tightly. The trainer forces him back to place with the collar and cord. Few dogs have the courage to break shot after two or three experiences with the collar applied in this manner.

If the dog is self-willed and obstinate above the ordinary, it is better to engage the assistance of a clear-headed friend to do the shooting, while the trainer devotes all his attention to the dog. Play to give the dog every opportunity to break shot, and let him go to the full length of the check cord as often as he will do so. If he at length hesitates to break, the trainer by feigning to break shot himself may encourage him to do so, but at every offense he is brought back to place with a pull of the collar, and if necessary he is still further punished with the whip. The most resolute dog will not persist in lawless breaking away under such treatment, and it has the further advantage of being lasting in its effects.

CHAPTER XIV

RETRIEVING

ALTHOUGH in America retrieving is made a part of the dog's field work, it is not a natural quality in the sense that pointing, reading, etc., are. There are those, however, who maintain that it is instinctive, and, moreover, that it is instinctively implanted in the dog's nature for the especial benefit of man.

The fact that an exceptional puppy will grasp a bird in his mouth on opportunity, in his first experience afield, and carry it with more or less directness to his master is cited as proof of its natural origin. The fact that the puppy will grasp the bird on his own account, even if his master is absent, is entirely ignored.

Whether in a wild or domestic state, if his prey is of a size which permits of his doing so the dog frequently carries it to his home. That he should at- tempt to carry it when in the presence of his master has therefore no special significance as an instinct whose purpose is the furtherance of his master's interests.

When the puppy first grasps the bird and makes what is termed a natural retrieve his every expression and purpose denote that the act has an entire reference to himself. His eyes glare with the triumph of possession; he grasps the bird with unnecessary firmness, oftentimes rolling and crushing it in his mouth, and he goes near to where his master stands as being the most secure and restful place under the circumstances. He would do precisely the same thing when he ceased work and wished to rest. At the juncture when the dog is near to him the trainer interposes, and by intimidation and restraint robs him, as it were, of his prey. If he is of mild or timid disposition he may yield his prize to his trainer at the first stern word or act in reference to it. Under similar circumstances he would in like manner desist from any other purpose or act in which he was engaged. But if the puppy is left to his own pleasure in the matter, he retains possession of the bird, lies down in a place to his liking and proceeds to devour it.

The mere picking up of the bird in the presence of the trainer and the success of the latter in plundering the dog of his prey are exceedingly limited data on which to found a theory that the act of retrieving is instinctive. Intelligent retrieving in the service of the gun is the result of education. If the dog retrieved naturally for the benefit of man he would exhibit and maintain a constant purpose of doing so, instead of a consistent purpose to possess and eat the bird. Furthermore, it would seem that if the dog retrieved naturally for man, the latter would know instinctively why the dog pointed and retrieved, but man has to be taught these things before he knows them.

Some dogs, it is true, learn to retrieve much more quickly than others, and take a great interest and delight in it. But this may be said of any other work imposed on the dog by man.

The average dog is easily susceptible to praise or flattery, and if he is skillfully handled in this respect he will do many things of no special interest or benefit to himself other than the vain gratification which he feels from evoking the approbation of his master. His keenness of observation and discrimination in determining what acts are pleasing and what are displeasing to the latter are purely matters of mental discernment.

The fact that almost any dog, whether he be cur or well bred, may be taught to retrieve indicates that the act is not a matter of instinct peculiar to setters and pointers. When done with any degree of finish and intelligent purpose it is an educational act quite as much as is the act of shooting the bird when displayed by his master. Incidentally, is it not strange that the dog should instinctively retrieve the bird which his master has learned to shoot, not instinctively, but by skill derived from education? It would seem that instinct would work alike in respect to both man and dog.

Dogs, as individuals, whether pointers or setters, vary greatly in their aptness for retrieving. Some manifest the greatest delight in it, and in fact in any other act within their compass which wins the approval of their masters, or which is associated with capturing prey; others perform in an indifferent or perfunctory manner, while still others detest and rebel against it heartily.

As a general proposition, by far the greater number of pointers and setters may be taught to retrieve with some degree of satisfactory performance. However, a dull nose, weak intellect or constitutional indolence will affect the dog's performance adversely in this respect as they will in all the other parts of his field work.

As a matter of good training it is much better to defer all attempts to teach retrieving till the dog's second season. When the teacher combines retrieving with the dog's other field schooling he retards instead of advances it.

The disadvantages consequent to retrieving are as

follows: Nearly all puppies and, indeed, many old dogs take an unbounded pleasure in capturing their prey. Each one has a keen desire to have individual possession of it. In their over-eagerness to be the first to the dead bird and gain possession of it they forget or disregard their training or obedience, so far as it refers to steadiness to the gun.

The desire to retrieve incites the dog to break shot: to be riotous when drawing on birds instead of being careful, and to lawless casting about after the gun is fired, in search of a real or imaginary dead bird, the report of the gun having to him but that one significance. The energetic efforts of the trainer at such junctures avail but little. The dog furiously charges about to find the bird. When at length the trainer gets control of him, his mind is still filled with the ardent desire and purpose to find the bird, and if freed he again begins his riotous search.

If at length the trainer, by energetic effort, gets control of him and leads him away a quarter of a mile, more or less, from the place where the dead bird is supposed to be, when released the puppy returns and persistently searches for it till he is pleased to desist, regardless of his handler's whistling and ordering in the meantime. At every report of the gun the puppy's misbehavior is amplified or modified, accordingly as the circumstances permit. If there are scattered birds about, his riotous charging is sure to flush them all, while he, heedless or oblivious of them, is absorbed in the one idea and effort to possess the dead bird.

This lawlessness, incorporated as a part of his field work, complicates matters seriously and harmfully. It lowers the standard of all his work as it relates to the service of the gun. The idea of possession constantly incites him to lawless alertness. The real or imaginary dead bird is ever an inducement to independent and lawless effort.

If the dog has been properly schooled the first sea- son, he is steady to shot and wing, besides having acquired an interest in working for the success of the gun. In the second season, retrieving, then, may be taught as a special branch, the dog having a preparatory good schooling to steadiness in his work to the gun as a finder. It requires no argument to prove that it is easier and better to perfect the dog in the first as a finding dog one season, and second as a retriever the ensuing season, than it is to attempt to perfect him in both branches at the same time.

Nevertheless, some dogs will exhibit all the undesirable traits enumerated ; other dogs one or more of them, while others, again, may engage in retrieving with pleasing precocity. As a general proposition the majority of dogs may be educated into being good retrievers, while a part may be educated into excellent ones.

Dogs of superior "bird sense" learn to engage in all the details of field work with an intelligent comprehension of what constitutes proper effort and action.

Notwithstanding the disadvantages which are likely to accrue when the dog is used both as a finder and retriever, the demands of sport as conducted in America require that he be so used. The average American sportsman owns but one or two dogs, and he desires that they serve him as finders. He has neither the time nor inclination to bother with a dog whose sole specialty is retrieving, and as a matter of economy some sportsmen would not consider that such dog's services counterbalanced the extra expense.

The average American sportsman has but a few days of shooting each season, and therefore his one dog in his service must be broadly proficient. While the dog may not be so good a finder if he retrieves, nor so good a retriever if he finds, a compromise may be established which will insure at least passable performance in both finding and retrieving, thus affording to the shooter the advantages of both.

Moreover, two dogs, the one a finder, the other a retriever, could not be handled at the same time by the average American sportsman, who, as a rule, finds quite enough difficulty in handling one dog at a time, Without a retriever, the success and pleasure of a day's shooting are materially impaired. Birds which fall in heavy weeds or grass or bushes are extremely difficult to find, and such as fall in mud or marshes, though in plain sight, are gathered with much difficulty and discomfort. When the shooter does his own retrieving a large percentage of dead and wounded birds and much time are lost.

As to the specific injuries to the work of the dog employed as a finder-retriever, they are as follows: The best manner of seeking live birds, in respect to the manner in which the dog uses his nose, is distinctly different from the best manner of using it in retrieving. The manner of finding is with a high nose, and therewith the dog cannot go to the birds too quickly consistently with steady performance.

His work then is on both bevies and single birds. As a retriever his work is entirely on single birds. He has a puzzling single trail to follow if the bird is wounded, and none at all if the bird is dead. To best find the wounded or dead bird it is essential tha he carry his nose close to the ground and trail slowly and this manner of retrieving the average dog learns. Unfortunately, this manner may be user after a time by the dog when seeking live birds, thus using the one manner whether seeking or finding.

It is comparatively easy to mar the best manner in which the dog uses his nose in finding, and when so marred it is beyond the power of the trainer to correct it.

CHAPTER XV

THE NATURAL METHOD

THE term "natural method" is a misnomer. It is distinctly misleading in its significance, for instead of being a natural manifestation, the vanity and pleasure of the dog are catered to by the trainer from start to finish inducing retrieving. The dog's self- interest is thus in a manner the basis of the trainer's lessons and success.

To the dog the lessons in this method are moments of mere delightful play. They are combined with flattery and petting by the trainer, which inflate the dog's body and spirit with pride and delight. His performance being thus dependent on his own pleasure, his advancement in retrieving, as a serious work, or, indeed, whether he advances well or not at all, is accordingly exceedingly uncertain. His own whimsical inclination is always the dominant factor. He engages in the lesson with ardor if he feels in a frolicsome mood, or disdainfully ignores it if he feels otherwise. It should more properly be called the amusement system, for such it really is.

It is, however, an important adjunct to the so-called force system, since the same flattery and petting have the same good effect on the dog when educated by that system, with the additional advantage that he must retrieve whether he is inclined to do so or not. Force properly applied establishes implicit and lasting obedience as groundwork. The amusement system added thereto supplements it and further appeals to the dog's self-interest by indulging him in amusement which is pleasurable. Later, when in actual field work, he comprehends the practical application of retrieving and delights in the material success which it brings. However, as it is generally considered as being a distinct method, it will be so treated in this work.

The "natural" method, so called, is not the best method. The "natural" retriever is rarely a finished retriever. Although termed a method it is inherently devoid of method. Under it, instead of governing the dog by method, the whim of the dog governs the trainer. It is crude and uncertain in its principles, since it is founded on the simple acts of the dog when voluntarily carrying the things in play for his own amusement.

The trainer, adopting the idea of amusement from the dog's standard, joins in the dog's frolic and, with a liberal bestowal of flattery to inveigle the dog into making a semblance of retrieving, terms such tentative efforts a method.

Briefly, the important faults of the system are that it is entirely inoperative if the dog has no inclination to play; that dogs vary greatly in their capacity for play when compared one with another, and that the same dog at different times varies widely in his moods concerning it ; that, though a dog may be inclined to play according to his own liking, he may not be inclined to play according to the liking of his trainer; that, being taught in play, many imperfections will necessarily be incorporated into his manner of retrieving; that he will never engage in it as a serious act entirely subject to the will of his trainer; that aged dogs, not being playful, cannot be taught by it, and that when at any time in his mature years the dog finds the work irksome or laborious to an unpleasant degree, he will quit it for good and all.

The natural retriever is rarely a finished retriever.

From the manner of his education he is predisposed to a hard mouth, to rolling the bird in his mouth or dropping and picking it up in a dilatory manner as he fetches it to his handler, and to dropping it on the ground several yards away instead of bringing it neatly to hand as he should.

If punished for any fault concerning it, he is very likely to quit retrieving. Punishment inflicted under any circumstances is by him understood to be for having the bird in possession at all, instead of for the faulty manner of retrieving it. In most instances, at some period of the natural retriever's life, he ceases to maintain his interest in retrieving and thereupon refuses to further engage in it.

Nearly all puppies have an uncontrollable desire to play. They will romp with each other or with such children as will join with them. The lone puppy, left to his own resources, derives great pleasure in fiercely carrying about and tossing an old shoe, or other available object, simulating attack and defense as if it were alive. He is not averse to engaging in play with his master, though the latter in his mature frolics oftentimes is too ponderous and calm as to deportment, and too conservative in his standards of play, to say nothing of his dangerous nature when irritated.

Play is the trait of the dog's character in this method which the trainer must utilize in schooling him to be a retriever. In its application there is no fixed or arbitrary rule. The trainer's tactfulness and the puppy's playfulness are the factors.

No serious punishment is permissible. Anything which stops the puppy from playing, stops the education at the same time. Disapproval may be shown when the puppy endeavors to rend or mouth the object to be retrieved, to the end that he may be checked more or less in his destructive tendency, but in that respect disapproval by word and manner is about as far as the trainer may safely venture.

By gradual and protracted stages the fun of the puppy is more or less imperfectly developed into the act of retrieving, by the exercise of an infinite degree of patience, persistency and good temper.

A palatable morsel, given to the dog when he has retrieved the object thrown out by the trainer, is a gratifying profit to him and therefore an appeal to his self-interest. However, when the edge is gone from his appetite, and therewith his self-interest is dormant for the time being, he is likely to be indifferent to the wishes of his trainer.

Before beginning the lessons, it is better to have the puppy's interest by engaging in play with him at numerous times during the preceding weeks, so that all his associations of ideas are anticipatory of amusement. Also, it is best to prohibit entirely all efforts to amuse him on the part of others. Thus the puppy from habit looks to his trainer and depends entirely upon him for his moments of pleasure; in fact, if no one else amuses him, he is ignorant of the fact that amusement exists apart from association with his trainer, and success will be according as the latter can bring himself down or up to the dog's standard of amusement.

A ball, pad or old glove makes a fairly good object on which to practice the dog in retrieving. It is better to wash them frequently when used, as, from be slavering and rolling on the ground, they quickly become soiled and offensive. An object with iron nails in it, so that the dog cannot bite it, is best, but, unfortunately, such object the dog refuses to hold in his mouth. Iron, when against the dog's teeth, is especially repugnant to him.

In the first lessons the trainer permits the dog to exercise his own pleasure. He is building up an interest in the sport which later is to become a business. When the dog is habituated to play, he teasingly waves the object to and fro before the dog's eyes in a challenge for him to seize it.

This the dog is keen to accept. While he is endeavoring to seize it, it is thrown alluringly out a few yards away, and he eagerly scrambles after it, grasps it in his mouth and struts about spiritedly in the pride of possession. If the trainer endeavors to get it, the puppy by pantomime banters him to get possession if he can do so, and by wily devices evades him as much as possible when he comes too near.

At length by craft and intimidation the trainer again gets possession of the object and throws it out as before. And thus the play proceeds, lesson by lesson, till from habit and deference to mild authority the puppy obeys the order to "Fetch," which is always uttered when the object is thrown out, so that this command is associated with the act of fetching.

The erratic faultiness which the puppy will display from the beginning should be corrected as positively and as soon as possible, consistently with holding his interest and effort. For instance, when he retrieves the object and the trainer is endeavoring to take it from him, he will hold it tightly in his mouth; if the trainer pulls on it forcefully he holds it the tighter, all of which has a tendency to make him hard- mouthed. If the trainer holds him by the collar with the right hand and grasps the object with his left, he can with the collar hold the dog in place so that he cannot exert any force on the object. Then he with his foot pinches the toes of the puppy while holding him kindly but firmly in place, at the same time uttering the command, "Give." In a few lessons the puppy will associate this command with a pain in his toes, and the act of opening his mouth and releasing the object he will associate with the avoidance of pain: thereupon he will open his mouth to release the object when he hears the command. Thus, "Fetch" denotes that he is to retrieve the object, and "Give" denotes that he is to release it when he has brought it to hand.

The results of this "method" are much as they happen to be. The lessons are continued through weeks and months, from the time the puppy is three or four months old till he matures. With age he becomes less frivolous. Month by month he is less playful, because it is the natural evolutionary development from youth to maturity: Many repetitions of the retrieving act become habitual, and what he at first did by way of amusement he may at last do by way of deference to the trainer, to a habit of life, to a desire to win approbation, and to a material self-interest in the way of food rewards, or to all combined.

After the puppy has reached a stage of advancement in which he will fetch the object with some degree of regularity and certainty, the trainer should direct his efforts toward schooling the puppy to carry the object without mouthing it. If he acquires a hard mouth, shown by closing tightly on the object or chewing it, there is no certainty that the fault can ever be cured. In actual retrieving, a hard-mouthed retriever is worse than none at all. He mutilates and destroys more birds than his services are worth.

To enforce steadiness it is better to make the lessons pertaining to it quite distinct from the other retrieving lessons. The trainer ties a rope three or four feet long to the puppy's collar so that he can control him easily, and, placing the object in his mouth, he forces him to hold it without biting it.

If the puppy is particularly predisposed to bite it, the object may be prepared with nails in it, as mentioned under the head of the force system. The object thus protected is placed in the puppy's mouth, and he is forced to keep it therein whether he is pleased to do so or not, but all is done with kindness and firm deliberation.

The lesson should be conducted without frightening him. If he ejects the object from his mouth, it should quickly be returned and by quiet coercion he should be forced to retain it.

He is next required to carry it steadily in his mouth while the trainer leads him about. These lessons are persisted in day after day till the puppy will carry the object without mouthing it.

When teaching him to carry steadily, the order "Steady" may be uttered every time he attempts to roll or chew the object, coincidently with a jerk on the collar to force him to desist, and in time he will learn that the order signifies that he is to avoid working his jaws upon the object he is retrieving.

There will be some unpleasant features to the puppy in these lessons, but if he is treated kindly as to manner, though firmly as to practice, he will not remember them long, and, being in separate lessons, he will not associate them with the main theme of retrieving.

As before intimated, the length of time required to teach retrieving by the natural method is from puppyhood to maturity. A few families of dogs, intelligent, deferential and vain by nature, take kindly to retrieving. However, when taught by the natural method, they rarely make a finished performance, and display all their peculiar selfish idiosyncrasies in their work.

After the puppy displays some steadiness and finish in retrieving the pad, or whatever other object is used, the wing or tail feathers of a common barnyard chicken may be tied to it, so that he will be accustomed to grasping them with his mouth. Although no dog hesitates to grasp them when they are on a bird which he himself has captured, many dogs manifest a persistent repugnance to them when they are attached to an object to be retrieved. So great is their dislike for them that the trainer may find it necessary to place the feathery object in the puppy's mouth and force him to carry it about, lesson after lesson, till by familiarity his repugnance is worn out. He is further schooled in fetching the feathered object till he will do so reliably.

CHAPTER XVI

THE FORCE SYSTEM

As THE term "force system" suggests, it is a system of teaching the dog retrieving, which, in part, s accomplished by the exercise of force. As a title, it, too, is misleading in its significance, since force is used only in the elementary stages of the lessons, and then to a limited degree.

The force, as applied, is for the purpose of causing pain to the dog. The absence of pain is so associated with certain acts that he commits them mechanically to avoid it. Pain of itself teaches the dog nothing whatever in the way of intelligent and positive retrieving. Its scope, however, is quite sufficient to enable the trainer to lay a firm elementary groundwork upon which the educational retrieving superstructure may be built.

When left to the exercise of his own will in the use of his mouth, the dog is predisposed to harshly grasp such objects as he closes it upon, Under the schooling of the natural system, the manner in which he uses it is practically beyond the control of the trainer. Indeed, his schooling, under that system, has a tendency to develop a hard mouth rather than to preserve a tender one.

In the "force system," the dog's manner of using his mouth is under the direct control of the trainer. Tender grasping of the object to be retrieved is a feature of it from the beginning. The dog notes that when he has the object in his mouth pain ceases. The manner in which the dog uses his mouth to the end that pain may be avoided, and that which he uses when impelled by natural impulse, are quite distinct. The one is gentle, the other forceful.

If cruelty is inflicted by any instrument which causes pain to the dog, the trainer should not, by any sophism, assume that the cruelty is inherent in such instrument. The cruelty, when it exists, comes from the application of the punishment.

Pain can be caused without any injury whatever to the dog. When the trainer loses his temper and mutilates and shocks his dog, he should not for a moment imagine that the origin of the cruelty is in the collar. The latter being absent, his boot, club, shotgun and whip would be quite likely to come into use, and are then cruel instruments, solely because they are so applied in a cruel manner by a cruel man.

To teach the dog to retrieve from the effects of pain, some trainers pinch the toes, the ears, the nose, or apply the whip or collar. The latter has the special advantage of direct control over the dog's mouth while the pain is inflicted. Pinching 1 the mouth hampers him in the use of it. When the pain is inflicted by the other means enumerated, the dog's mouth is under but little control, hence the progress is less positive and less complete.

In the application of force, intelligence, kindness, sympathy for the dog in his efforts to perform the desired act, good temper and a knowledge of dog nature are essential to the best success. An ignorant man can apply more force, but he should not confound his senseless punishing ability with true dog training. To cause pain is a limited aid to training; it is not the training itself.

Retrievers trained after the "force system" are finished

performers of their work. By virtue of this system, they have undergone a discipline which left their dislikes and objections unconsidered. They have recollections of implicit obedience only as a means of avoiding pain. Their impressions concerning it are lifelong.

A tender mouth can be insured under this system if the trainer has ordinary skill. Also, under it, the dog can be taught to retrieve whether he is old or young. The discipline further conquers and subjugates him in a general way, without impairing his independence or breaking his spirit.

Any hurry in the training sh6uld be carefully avoided. The dog must have ample time to comprehend the purposes of his trainer, and to remember what associated acts free him from pain.

After the dog will pick up the object and fetch it mechanically, the so-called natural method is applied, and the dog is then petted, flattered and rewarded in his work, to the end that his enthusiasm and self-interest may be evoked.

In the force system, the progress may be roughly differentiated into stages namely, that in which the dog merely opens his mouth mechanically when he hears the command "Fetch!" as a preventive or avoidance of pain; that in which he will actively engage in an effort to grasp the object when h hears the command, if the object is held on a level with his mouth, a few feet in front of him ; that in which he will follow it up and pick it out of the hand of the trainer, or off the ground or floor, knowing then fully that the act if completed will free him from pain ; that in which the attempt is made to teach the dog to pick up an object off the floor or ground without the fear of the collar. If each stage has been thoroughly inculcated, but little, if any, difficulty will be encountered in steady advancement.

He further must be schooled to go after the object when it is thrown to a distance.

If at first he fights the collar, the trainer lets him do so at the end of the check cord till he entirely desists.

A corncob is a good object to school the dog on in his first lessons. It is not repugnant to him; it is shaped so that he can conveniently hold it in his mouth, and a clean one can be conveniently used at every lesson.

The first lessons should be given in a room, free from disturbing noises and the presence of spectators. The dog should face diagonally across his trainer on the right side, so that he will be facing the object held in the trainer's left hand in front of him.

The running free end of the collar rests on top of the dog's neck. A piece of half-inch rope, about three feet long, is fastened to it. The trainer firmly grasps the collar close up to the dog's neck, holds the cob close in front of the dog's nose, and gives the command "Fetch," pulling firmly on the collar at the same time. If the dog opens his mouth to cry out, the cob is then instantly slipped into his mouth, at the same time slackening on the collar and stopping all pain.

The first pull or two will determine the character of the pupil. He may be tenderly responsive to the force, or grimly sulky and mute, or disposed to fight. If he will not open his mouth to a jerk of the collar, the trainer catches it close up to the dog's neck, twists his hand outward, thereby drawing the collar tightly and shutting off the dog's wind partially, and forcing him to open his mouth, and the collar at the same time is loosened to end the pain.

If he shows fight, the whip is administered while he is held to the punishment with the collar, and this is continued till all the fight is taken out of him.

After each command to "Fetch," with the corresponding pull on the collar and insertion of the cob in the dog's mouth, the trainer waits a few moments, soothing the dog to restore his confidence. When he holds it well, leave it in his mouth a few moments and praise him. If he eject it, replace it instantly in his mouth, at the same time giving him a sharp admonitory jerk.

His little weaknesses should be* studied, so that advantage may be taken of them. Make the first lessons short. There is plenty of time to teach the dog the accomplishment, and there are two things therewith to ever keep in mind namely, to avoid hurry and to keep in good temper. The dog must have time to comprehend the purposes of the trainer; to associate the command and pain with the act which will avoid the latter, and to memorize all the particulars which make up the lesson. When hurried or distressed from the confusion, he becomes overheated and holds his mouth open while panting, at which juncture he cannot close it on the cob without great distress.

Each lesson should end in a romp after the collar is removed, thereby completely restoring the dog's confidence, and making a pleasant ending to the lesson.

The first simple lessons should be continued till the dog will open his mouth promptly the moment that he hears the order "Fetch." The next stage is to teach him to step forward and grasp the cob when he hears the command. The dog is now brought into active instead of passive obedience. He must act instead of being acted upon. The trainer holds the cob about a foot in front of the dog's nose, gives the command "Fetch," at the same time jerking him forward sharply to the cob, which he is induced to seize, and which he will seize when within reach of it, if the preliminary lessons have been properly inculcated. These lessons teach the dog to advance forward for the cob when he hears the command.

When the dog has grasped the cob, or when he has in good faith attempted to do so and failed, the punishment should instantly cease.

When he quite realizes the virtue of the cob in his mouth in affording immunity from punishment, he will object to release it even when the trainer so desires, Its absence he learns after a time signifies that punishment impends. When he releases it, caress and reassure him. If he closes tightly on it and refuses to deliver it, no violence or impatience should be manifested. Grasp the cob in the left hand gently utter the command "Give," stepping on the toes of one of his forefeet at the same time. It is not necessary to pinch them severely. A gentle pressure will be quite sufficient to accomplish the purpose. The order "Give" will be promptly obeyed after a few lessons given in this manner.

Up to this stage the dog, as a general rule, acts

mechanically. He steps forward and puts his mouth on the cob because the act saves him from pain. He has not perception sufficient to enable him to comprehend that it is necessary for him to lower his head if the trainer holds the cob near the floor in front of him. At this stage the dog's natural inclination to grasp a moving object may be aroused, and then he may follow it up and grasp it on his own initiative.

When this is evoked, the rest of the training is easy. The trainer caters to the dog's inclination to make it an amusement. The command "Fetch" is given, the cob is wiggled teasingly close to his nose, and when he follows after it, it is moved two or three feet further on, till he overtakes and closes his mouth on it.

Some dogs soon develop an enthusiastic inclination to enter into the matter as an amusement at this stage, but no more playfulness should be permitted than is necessary to make the lessons cheerful and successful. The grave and gay should be properly blended.

If the dog, however, refuses to be amused, the trainer lowers the cob an inch or two below the level of the dog's mouth, and forces him to grasp it in the new position. Lesson after lesson the cob is lowered little by little as the dog becomes proficient, till at length he will take it from the trainer's hand held at the level of the floor.

At this stage the dog in most instances requires extra patience in conducting his lessons. He has been habituated to associating the cob and hand together, and has looked to the moving hand as the thing to follow when ordered to "Fetch." Hence, when the trainer places the cob on the floor, uttering the command and taking his hand away, the dog is likely to follow the moving hand instead of grasping the cob. To overcome this, the trainer places the cob on the floor in front of the dog, utters the command, and then moves his hand to one side an inch or two only. If the dog goes to the hand, it is then an easy matter to direct his attention to the cob.

As the lessons progress, the hand may be moved away to greater and greater distances, as the dog more and more learns that the cob is the matter under consideration. He can grasp it with much greater ease and quickness, thereby advancing better in his training, if two sticks about three inches in length are placed at right angles in each end of it, thus forming a kind of saw- horse.

After the dog will pick up the cob when placed on the floor close in front of him, another stage may be attempted. The cob is tossed gently a foot or two in front of him, care being taken to have him see it when tossed. He is prompted to go for it by kind inducement, if possible; if he refuses, he is forced forward with the collar.

A longer and lighter check cord may be used at this stage, accordingly as the dog broadens in the scope of his work.

A great deal of difficulty will be encountered if the preceding lessons have been hurried, or if they have been imperfectly taught, either or both of which are quite probable in the first attempts of the amateur. If progress is made in a proper manner, each stage is easy and certain, with the infliction of little pain or
none at all. If the trainer cannot conduct the spike-collar lessons in a proper manner, it is much better for himself and infinitely better for the dog that the system be

abandoned.

If at any time the dog shows a disposition to bite the cob, some slim ten-penny nails should be tied half an inch apart, lengthwise to it, so that its surface is protected by the iron. This, against his teeth, is abhorrent to him. He will at first refuse to grasp it, but when forced to do so will carry it, and with exceeding tenderness.

Next he is given lessons in retrieving a dead bird. It is better to protect it with nails at first, both to prevent him from pinching it with his teeth, to associate it with pain to the teeth if grasped too hard, and to insure a habit of tenderness from the first to the last attempts in retrieving birds. He will require a number of lessons to perfect him in this.

Next he should be taught to refrain from going after the object till he is ordered to do so. It is better to make him "Drop," and so remain till he hears the order to "Fetch."

In the lessons teach one order at a time. Do not order the dog to "Fetch/' and as he starts to obey do not command him to "Drop," or "Toho," etc. Such training balks and confuses him. One order and obedience to it are sufficient at one time. Good progress on the part of the dog is consequent to industry and good sense on the part of the trainer. If the good sense is absent, the dog should be held blameless. Each part in detail should be perfected. The dog should be required to remain passive till he is given the command "Fetch," then to go directly to the bird, pick it up gently and quickly, and return in a direct line to the trainer. No nosing of the bird, nor dawdling on the way, either when going to or coming with it, should be tolerated. The bird should be delivered in hand, and released instantly on the order "Give."

The retriever should be thoroughly proficient in all the yard lessons before any attempts are made at actual field work, and then great care should be exercised to guard against two dogs attempting to retrieve the same bird, or against interference with a good retriever by a partly broken dog. A thoroughly trained dog may be demoralized in a few moments by such bad management.

Some preliminary training may be given the dog afield, which in a way will be of value in marking the flight of birds and in "seeking dead." The cob is shown to him, then thrown in the air far away, where he can see it and mark its flight. He is not permitted to go after it till he is ordered to "Fetch." He will then have some difficulty in finding it, and will rake the ground about with his nose in an effort to catch scent of it. The lessons may be varied by throwing the cob to the opposite side of walls, fences, bushes, etq., thus enabling the dog to see part of its flight, but preventing him from seeing it land. When assisting the dog to search for it, the trainer utters the command "Seek," or "Find," or whatever other command he may fancy, at the same time affecting earnestness in searching for it himself. In this manner, after a sufficient number of lessons, the dog will mark the cob's" flight quite accurately, will find it with reasonable quickness, and will learn the significance of the commands pertaining to searching for it.

These lessons should be given in moderation, as they have a decided tendency to develop the carriage of a low nose, a style of work which should be discouraged as much as possible in a dog used as a bird finder.

In respect to actual field work, after the dog is perfected in retrieving, the trainer should ever bear in mind that all retrievers are not alike, even when perfectly educated, and that circumstances alter cases. Dogs vary greatly in strength. A dog physically small and delicate might be an excellent retriever of quail and woodcock, and yet be a poor retriever of prairie chickens, owing to their extra weight.

The dog at best, owing to his construction, is not a good weight carrier. Moreover, when required to retrieve large birds on a hot day, he, if panting violently, may be forced to drop the bird so that he can breathe, etc. The shooter should have some consideration and charity for his dog under such circumstances. He has consideration for himself, as shown by his voluminous excuses for missing a bird, as shown by the plea that he didn't know it was loaded, or by resting in the shade when uncomfortably warm, etc.

However well a dog may perform in his yard lessons, they cannot be accepted as final data concerning his actual work afield. Carrying an object to hand is not all of retrieving. he dog must have a keen intelligence, so that he will understand how to work intelligently to the gun ; he must have a keen nose, so that he may be able to trail running birds to their hiding places, and locate the dead ones; he should have a pleasant, tractable disposition and take pleasure in his work ; he should be able to mark and remember the flight of wounded birds, and also be able to distinguish between the flight of a wounded bird and one which is not.

The finished retriever does his work expeditiously and accurately, because he knows what to do and how to do it.

The poor retriever knows but little more than how to fetch a bird when he comes across it. All the intelligent cognizance of details is lost to him.

Retrieving ducks and geese is too laborious work for the average pointer and setter. Furthermore, their constitution is not sufficiently strong to with stand the shock and exposure incident to it, if they are used as retrievers of wildfowl for any length of time.

CHAPTER XVII

GUN-SHYNESS AND BLINKING

THE dog flees from the sight of a gun or the report of it simply because he is afraid, and this display of fear is called gun-shyness. It is one of the most common educational troubles which embarrass and obstruct the efforts of the amateur. It is commonly the result of his own faulty attempts at training, or the acts of those who are equally thoughtless.

The novice, in most cases, proceeds on a wrong theory in his endeavor to accustom the dog to the report of the gun. His own knowledge of it is generally and unconsciously made the standard by which to measure the puppy's knowledge.

Generally the trainer fails to consider that the puppy is wholly ignorant concerning the uses of the gun, and that its terrorizing reports, which cause fear in many boys, also may be to the puppy a cause of intense fear. If the trainer would keep in mind that his own early boyhood, with its timidity, ignorance and immaturity, is a better standard by which sympathetically to understand and school the puppy, he rarely, if ever,
would have cases of gun-shyness.

Men of excellent sense in other matters assume as a matter of course that a dog and gun were made as natural corollaries of each other, and hence could be used together as if they were litter brothers. Any- thing short of success in the application of the theory is ascribed to the dog's nature

To punish a dog for his fears adds to and confirms him in them. The fact that so many dogs are cured of gun-shyness is positive proof that they never would have been afraid of the gun if they had been properly accustomed to it from the beginning. It is a self-evident fact that if a dog's shyness of the gun can be allayed, after he has acquired a fear of it, by proper treatment, before he has any fears of it at all he can be familiarized with its use, without causing him alarm. A little care at first in familiarizing the puppy with the noise of the gun will often times save many weeks or months of later trouble, and add so much more to his usefulness.

However, the trainer will have cases of gun-shy-ness to cure, resulting either from his own mistakes or those of others, and therefore it is necessary that he should know the best methods of treatment for it. Some apparently mild cases persist to a discouraging degree, while under favorable circumstances some bad cases may be cured readily. Nevertheless, the degree of shyness exhibited is no criterion of the length of time required to effect a cure, nor is there any arbitrary method by which a cure may be effected.

Highly nervous dogs are easily made gun-shy if the trainer has been so thoughtless as to frighten them by heedlessly firing the gun. Indeed, the dogs of steadiest nerves can easily be made gun-shy if the report of the gun is associated with pain, as when punishment is inflicted in training the dog to drop to shot, or for breaking shot, etc. If the dog, furthermore, is afraid of his trainer, any unusual or extra serious acts of the latter are regarded with alarming apprehension, and evoke purpose to seek safety by flight.

Gun-shy dogs pursue quite distinct ways in seeking safety from the gun or avoiding it. Some run away entirely, either returning home or going afield, or taking advantage of the opportunity to self-hunt; others seek the first place which affords concealment, and tremblingly hide therein; or, terror-stricken, others may lie down a few yards away and curl up apathetically; or they may range at a safe distance from the handler and outside of his control. Some will be afraid at the sight of a gun; others will show no fear of it till it is placed at the shoulder as if to fire it, while others, again, have fear only of the report.

There are three essentials to be observed in curing gun-shyness namely, the dog must not be permitted to run away, the gun must be used in a manner which impresses as having no reference to him at all, and the trainer must have his pupil's confidence and affection, for if the pupil is afraid of both gun and trainer (gun-shy and trainer-shy), the prospect of a cure is not hopeful. Fear of the trainer, if such there be, must first be allayed before any successful attempt can be made to cure the dog's gun-shyness.

There are different methods of cure. If the dog is inclined to run away when his gun fears are excited, he should be taken into an enclosed yard, from which he cannot escape. The trainer should assume a kind, careless, nonchalant air, and seem to be interested in any other thing than his pupil. Above all, the serious, portentous air, such as the trainer has when he is about to give the puppy a thrashing, should be avoided, although such, nevertheless, is quite likely to be the air that the amateur will assume. By sternly concentrating the attention on a dog, and advancing on him with more or less hostility of manner, the bravest dog will become fearful of harm.

If the dog will not bolt at the report of the gun, no precautions against running away are necessary but whether in field or yard, the gun as a factor of the lesson should be kept in abeyance for a while. The effort should be directed toward making the incident commonplace and unimportant. There should be as much of the pleasurable and as little of the painful as possible in it. A few palatable morsels to eat, some gentle patting on the head and kind words of approval bestowed on the pupil will not be amiss at different timely stages of the lesson. After a time, when the pupil is not so apprehensive of it, a cap is snapped, and the trainer looks at anything other than the dog at this juncture. He can see what the dog is doing without looking directly at him. The latter, when he hears the report, is likely to scrutinize the trainer closely, and if he detects no purpose referring to himself, he passes the incident by as a matter of no importance. On the other hand, let the trainer look hard at the dog, and impress upon him that all the alarms are directed at him, and the matter is made worse instead of better. If he runs to a corner and curls up in fancied security, he must be brought gently back, and the same deliberate procedure is continued.

Another method, often successful, is to place the dog's food in its regular place at the regular time, and then to shoot at a reasonable distance away when the dog begins to eat. If he bolts into his kennel, the food is quietly removed, and none given again till the next meal time, when the lesson is again repeated as at first. In time his hunger will become so ravenously importunate that he will appease it regardless of all fears. The noise of the gun coincidentally will have a grateful significance and a pleasant association, so that the fears will give way to delighted eagerness. As a matter of course, under this method the dog's liberty is restricted at all times, otherwise he would seek food independently.

If the dog is a confirmed bolter, it is better to take him at once into the open field for his lessons. He must be prevented from running away, and hence the spike collar and check cord come into useful play at this juncture. They do not in the least allay his fears of the gun, nor have they any inherent powers of cure concerning it. They simply prevent or deter him from running away, and thus prevented he must be, else a cure cannot be effected. Then, shooting with judgment and exhibiting kindness, an unconcerned manner, and a judicious bestowal of rewards will affect a cure in the majority of cases.

Dogs have been cured by taking them to a trap shooting tournament and chaining them in a safe place near-by the shooters. Neither dog nor man can remain continuously in a state of fright, whether the danger is real or imaginary. Continuous firing, hour after hour, merely wears out the dog's fright, and he becomes accustomed to it from habit.

If the dog has ordinary courage and sense, the cure is sometimes effected in the field in a moment. If he has a desire to pursue birds, he may be led on a long cord into a field where they are numerous, and when one attracts his attention it is shot, if not protected by law, and he is permitted to capture it. Again, if he can in any way be induced to chase a rabbit, if the trainer can shoot it ahead of him while he is in close pursuit, a cure is in most instances affected then and there.

The company of an old, steady dog is at all times reassuring, regardless of his breed or special hunting proclivities. A rabbit dog, however, is likely to be the best assistant. Nothing so excites the spirit of the chase in a dog as to see or hear another dog in full cry after a rabbit.

A gun-shy dog should never be worked on game birds before he is fully cured of his fault otherwise the chances are great that he becomes bird-shy and a blinker. If he has both faults, he must have exceptionally good qualities if he is worth the attempt to cure him.

A blinker is cured by kind treatment, by permitting him to eat the entrails of the birds which are shot, and by ignoring any faults and errors of which he may be guilty. Sometimes the one who caused the blinking can never cure it, and therefore it is necessary to place the pupil in the charge of another trainer. Much has been written on the heredity of gun-shyness, but most of the writers on it have succeeded better in proving that they were not quite familiar with what constitutes heredity than that the dog's fears were transmitted. Dogs of a highly nervous and excitable temperament, with a silly mentality, show alarm at any strange noises, whether caused by the gun or anything else.

CHAPTER XVIII

THE TOOLS OF TRAINING

THE whip, whistle, spike collar and check cord are all the instruments the trainer needs to perfect the dog in his education for work to the gun.

Both whip and spike collar have been denounced as cruel instruments. They are cruel or not, according as they are used. The cruelty therefore is in their application, which is a manifestation of the trainer's purposes.

If the trainer cannot use the spike collar without being cruel, it is better for him to entirely forego its use, as it is better also to forego any attempts at training if he cannot control his temper.

When properly applied, the collar inflicts pain without mutilation. It serves a useful purpose, and its use therefore can be justified on that score. Breaking the colt to harness, which at first hurts him, or breaking the ox to the yoke, inflicts certain degrees of pain, yet if not carried to unnecessary lengths no one considers that cruelty is inflicted. One or two cuts from a heavy whalebone whip raises welts on the side of the roadster, and causes a greater intensity of suffering than there would be occasion to inflict in all the lessons of the average retriever.

Anger and violence result in cruelty. When they are exhibited, the trainer is such in name only. He then is unfit to teach, and incapacitates the pupil.

The best training collar, though called a spike collar, is a combination of both spike and choke collar. Its construction should be simple and its material of the best. The leather should be medium weight harness leather, without sponginess or flaws of any kind. For convenience in use, the collar is made in two parts.

The longer part should be from 22 inches to 24 inches in length by i| inches in width. An iron oblong, sufficiently large to allow the free end of the strap to play through it, is sewed in one end of the strap. If the ring were used it would allow the strap to twist around; the oblong prevents it from doing so. The spikes, six in number, are screwed through steel plates on one side of the strap, two to a plate, and are secured by nuts screwed on them on the opposite side of the strap. The spikes should project inwardly about one-half inch. The points should have a bevel of about 45 degrees, so that they will hurt without cutting or puncturing the skin. The shorter strap, 2 or 3 inches in length, has a square buckle at one end to buckle on the free end of the collar, and a ring is at the other end in which to fasten the check cord.

The whip is carried and used to punish the dog for any misbehavior in a general way. Its presence has a beneficial moral effect. While the dog enjoys the society of his master as a companion, he detests any servitude which conflicts with his own spontaneous actions or purposes, and he obeys many times for no other reason than that it is compulsory.

The presence of the whip and its significance do much to maintain discipline. For its moral effect, many trainers carry it fastened to the coat, where it is in sight at all times, and where it is instantly available when needed. The majority of trainers and shooters, however, carry it in the pocket. The kinds most in favor are flexible, so that they may be rolled up and stowed in a small compass.

Whips heavily loaded with iron or lead should never be used, as they are unpleasant to carry, and, as a slung-shot, are not at all needed in furtherance of the dog's education.

A silk or linen cracker on the end of the whip adds to its effectiveness. It also preserves the lash from wearing out. An admonitory crack of it often will serve to adjust the dog's efforts quite as well as a whipping.

The check cord serves a most useful purpose in keeping the dog under control at such times as he would misbehave or interfere if left to his own will, or run away if he is displeased or afraid. It also comes efficiently into use in many parts of the field and yard breaking.

A braided cord is the best. It does not require so much care in coiling it for the pocket, and it cannot untwist in the annoying manner peculiar to common rope.

The cord used to connect windows with their counterbalance serves admirably the purposes of a check cord. A one-quarter-inch line is quite large enough for all field purposes, although in the yard lessons a one-half-inch line, as being easier on the hands, may be preferable. The check cord should be as short as is consistent with affecting the desired purpose. If used beyond a certain length, which is variable, according to the special matter to be accomplished, it is more or less cumbersome and unmanageable. When not in use it should be coiled carefully, so that when one end is fastened to the dog's collar the rest of it will play freely without tangling or kinking.

The whistle serves as a great aid in handling the dog when he is seeking for prey. It should have a good tone, of medium pitch. Metallic whistles have a tendency to make the mouth sore, and when full of frost in cold weather are painful to the teeth and lips. For use, it is best suspended from near the hunting-coat collar in front by a string of sufficient length.

The senseless and continuous whistling practiced by some trainers and shooters should be studiously avoided. To the dog, the blasts have a meaning only when they are associated with definite ideas, and such he cannot have if the whistling is continuous. If the whistle is carried habitually in the mouth there is a great temptation to blow it unnecessarily, therefore it is better to keep it in the pocket until it is actually needed. Men who carry it in their mouths continuously are prone to acquire a drawn, anxious look, and are ever alert to blow it on the slightest pretext of setting the dog aright in his seeking. Probably nine out of ten of the blasts on the whistle are unnecessary, and therefore more or less harmful .Its only useful place in the management of the dog .at work is to turn him if taking a cast too wide; to attract his attention to a signal of the hand, which the shooter desires him to see, and to make him cease work and come in. A different note is used for the respective purposes, and once the note is definitely fixed upon, it should always be used in its proper relation and none other.

The trainer can use any note or combination of notes which he pleases, there being nothing especially conventional in this respect, although in a general way a long and short note are used to make the dog turn, a succession of short, sharp notes to attract his attention, and a prolonged whistle to call him in.

When trained for field trial purposes, some dogs are taught to work further out and go faster to blasts of the whistle, to the end that the whistling of the opposing handler may not check the dog's efforts.

CHAPTER XIX

FIELD TRIAL BREAKING AND HANDLING

IN field trial competition, a dog needs to do his best, and this he can do only when he has self-confidence, proper schooling, good spirits, and the stamina which comes from excellent physical condition.

A dog working alone in such a manner as pleases himself, and, perhaps, in a manner pleasing to the shooter, is then engaged quite differently from a matter of competition. Allowed to take his own time and methods he may do well ; but in competition his performance is relative, and therefore inferior if some other dog does better.

The field work of the dog, with its cramped subservience to the interests of the gun, and the work of the dog in field trial competition, are distinct, inasmuch as the pottering of the shooter and dog in actual work is largely eliminated.

There are shooters who hold that a field trial should be an exhibition of high-class fie!4 work as it is done in actual service to the gun afield. Such arguments are absurd. To hold a dog down to the restrictions imposed by actual work to the gun would vitiate all competition. The purpose of the competition is to try out the dog's powers to the utmost in the qualities that are essential in actual field work, and in the approved manner of field work, free from the obstructiveness of the shooter whose dominant idea is the capture of the bird rather than the degree of his dog's natural qualities.

The capture of the bird, by the way, is a difficult idea to

remove from the average shooter's field trial data. He cannot consider a race between two or more dogs without making the dead bird a standard of value

One season at field trials usually convinces the as-in-actual-field-work oracle that he is quite right, and the field trial world is quite wrong; in the second season he begins to learn something on the one hand and unlearn something on the other ; and, later on, if he has a reasonable degree of good sense, he learns to know that he did not know it all.

The term "natural qualities" is difficult to explain to the advocate of pure field work which is done in the interest of the gun, for the reason that it embodies a theory which runs counter to his prejudgments and prejudices. He generally attempts the *reductio ad absurdum* that "natural qualities" indicate an unbroken dog turned loose to run wild. As a matter of fact, the field trial dog needs to be broken to a certain useful degree, and while he competes after the manner of actual field work he is freed from its deadening burdens. The trotting horse is broken to harness and to obedience to voice and rein, yet he, in a race, is given the freest opportunity to display his natural qualities to their utmost. Why not insist that he should race to a farm cart so that his natural qualities would thereby be displayed "as in actual field work"?

The manner in which the horse races is not the manner in which he is driven on the road; the manner in which he is trained on the track is not the manner in which he is trained for road work; yet the natural qualities, the speed, stamina, intelligence, gameness, disposition, etc., which the horse displays in races are the qualities which are of service in actual road work, and when he is used in the latter service the manner of handling him is modified accordingly.

No sane man would think of driving his horse on the road if he were racing for a championship. Most men can talk sensibly in respect to the distinctions between a race horse and a cart horse, yet a large percentage of them would probably lose their good judgments when considering the differences between a field dog and a field trial dog, though the difference between them might be merely a matter of handling. Indeed, a clog might be both a field trial dog and a field dog, and not infrequently he is such. Few men can handle a race horse or field trial dog; not every man can handle the ordinary horse or dog, and some men cannot handle any kind of dog, for which they hold the dog blamable.

It is true that fast dogs have bolted at field trials, and it also is true that race horses have run away on the tracks when racing, but it would be erroneous to assume that such acts are considered standards of merit. And yet a dog of high-class natural qualities may commit a flagrant error and win race, not by virtue of having committed such error, but by virtue of being a better performer than his competitors, error and all considered. On the other hand, a dog may commit an error of such magnitude that it disqualifies him from further competition in the race in which he is engaged.

Field trials are conducted by intelligent, experienced gentlemen. They have all the experience and knowledge which come from * 'actual field work," with the added knowledge of what constitutes the principles of a competition and the best manner of conducting it.

177

In preparing a dog for a competition it therefore is better to act on the theory that he will engage in a race. Memories of what dear Star did on a memorable day when he made forty-nine or more points with birds to every point will not offset his inferior performance in competition. Not what he has done, but what he does do, is the only datum the judge considers.

To perform at his best, a dog must be in fine physical condition. His muscles must be hard and strong; his feet tough; his body free from fat and surplus flesh, all resulting from sufficient exercise in the preliminary weeks, combined with proper feeding and general good care. Furthermore, he must have ample practice on birds, so that he will be able to perform quickly and skillfully on them, Speedy work is essential, for one can easily understand that a dog which works on his birds sharply, accurately and intelligently will not give a slower dog any chance to score, however well the latter may be able to work if given more time. No forcing process serves to fit the dog for a field trial. Over-exercising to reduce fat, whipping to correct errors, etc., do not condition or prepare the dog. Soft flesh, thick wind and un-skillfulness are not corrected by hurry or pressure. Good, honest preparation and enough time are the essentials.

Without the necessary preparation no dog has other than an exceedingly remote chance in a field trial competition. Trusting to luck and to one's own ability to help the dog to win is trusting to a forlorn hope.

The judges are quite alive to what work is done independently by the dog and what is done by the assistance of his handler. They will make their estimates accordingly. This does not imply that skill is not necessary in handling a dog in a field trial, but it notes a distinction between skillfully handling a dog which is able to make a good competition and, on the other hand, endeavoring to assist one which is unfit to compete. Handling and assisting are different matters.

Sharp practice is now many years obsolete. Honesty and skillfulness are not in the least antagonistic. Any attempts at trickery are instantly detected by the modern judge, and if the offending handler escapes a reprimand on the spot he does not escape close surveillance thereafter and a disbelief in his honesty on the part of the judges, so that, in a way, he justly suffers a depreciation of character from any attempts at tricky handling.

The field trial dog is best developed by permitting him to self-hunt, or by conducting his training on a modification of it. In this manner his self-interest is stimulated to its utmost, consistent with a reasonable degree of work to the gun.

Some dogs work less keenly when restricted too closely in their work to the gun; others work in a slovenly, spiritless manner under such circumstances.

The greater self-interest the trainer can evoke in the dog, the greater will be the dog's effort to gratify it. This, in the main, can be done and maintained only by kindness and encouragement.

The chief considerations in a field trial are locating the birds; pointing them; backing the competing dog; "bird sense"; steadiness to point, wing and shot; judgment in speed and endurance in ranging.

The general wisdom of the dog, as manifested by his practical acts, is expressed by the term "bird sense." Any training over and above what brings out these qualities in a finished manner is redundant, and, from a competitive standpoint, tends toward harming the dog's chances rather than toward improving them. In seeking, finding, pointing, etc., the mind of the dog should be concentrated on the work which is recognized as competitive. If he makes his work secondary to the doings of his handler he is thereby hampered with considerations which are not competitive, and his performance as a contestant will be injured accordingly. In short, the field trial dog is trained specially to fit the conditions of a race. If he works out his ground with greater speed and more judgment, follows a trial with greater speed and precision, points his birds more truly than does his competitor, he will be doing practically all the work. His opponent then will seem \Q be doing nothing, for the work all being done before he can get to it, there is nothing for him to do. Contrary to the views held by some writers, great experience on game is no handicap to the field trial dog. It, on the contrary, gives him the knowledge which he needs in competition. He cannot be too knowing in all the details of field work. Great experience, however, may not be confounded with overwork or staleness, which is a decided factor in making a dog indifferent and unfit for his best performance. Experience, in a proper sense, never makes a dog less keen or less snappy in his work, but overwork will, to a certainty, make him so.

The essentials of a good field trial dog's performance are as follows: Staying out at his work industriously, and therefore never coming in to his handler till ordered to do so; beating out his ground with judgment that is to say, going from one to another of the places likely to serve as haunts or feeding grounds for the birds; locating the birds quickly and accurately after he catches the foot scent or the body scent; pointing them intelligently and stanchly, and backing only when it is necessary to do so; all being governed by a desire to be independent in action, and take the initiative whenever it is possible to do so. To be fitted naturally for such performance he must have speed, intelligence, stamina, enthusiasm and pluck, self-confidence, a good nose and a good disposition.

The preliminary fitting of the dog for field trial competition is a matter to keep in mind at all times. During the summer months he should be kept in reasonably good physical condition by exercise, good food and a wholesome place in which to sleep. His field work, beginning with short hunts, is gradually increased, till he is given all the work he can stand without lessening his enthusiasm and energy in it.

He should when at work be thrown entirely on his own resources, consistent with the conditions exacted by the competition.

If the dog has not the knowledge of how best to hunt his ground or go to his birds, etc., before the race, during the race is a badly chosen time in which to teach or assist him. While the handler is endeavoring to help his dog to accomplish a certain act, the competing dog, more confident and able, may do it readily on his own initiative.

The information already presented in this work on the subject of a steadiness to shot, point, back and wing is applicable to the training of the field trial dog. He must be steady in the work which is designated as being competitive. Flushing intentionally or through erroneous judgment will be penalized to a certainty, although flushes under adverse conditions, such as running onto a bird down or across wind when the dog could not scent it, are rarely considered demerits.

The best manner of ranging, reading, pointing, etc., qualities treated fully in previous chapters, are essential to the field trial dog. They should be carefully developed to their best, for the fact that the dog is in a race instead of "an ordinary day's shooting" should ever be borne in mind, for to insist that the field trial should be conducted as an ordinary day's shooting is analogous to insisting that a horse race should be conducted as an ordinary day's farm work. In the one case, the dog displays the powers with which Nature endowed him, under the least restriction consistent with his control; in the other, he displays his powers as a menial habituated to the restrictions of servitude. It is better to give the dog as much preparation as possible near the scene of the trials, so that he may have experience on grounds similar to those of the field trials and become acclimated. Changes of water, climate, food, etc., not infrequently affect the dog's condition and the quality of his field work for several days or weeks. He never should be run longer than he maintains his best speed and effort.

An hour at first, once or twice a day, night and morning, when the dog is coolest, with a two-hour run every second or third day when he is in better condition, will serve to maintain the average good dog at his best field work. It is a mistake, on the other hand, to have a dog so highly keyed in speed that from an excess of animal spirits he will run so fast that he cannot do anything other than to pick out a course to run in. When so extended, he can- not use his nose to the best advantage, even if he can use it at all. For the trials which have longer heats than a half hour or hour, the matter of endurance must be more seriously considered and the preparation of the dog must aim to establish less speed and longer effort. His preparatory runs then are longer, to conform with the longer runs exacted in the competition wherein endurance is a factor.

Dogs vary greatly in their capacity for work; Some will perform well every day, while others; again, may not be equal to a satisfactory performance oftener than every other day. The idiosyncrasies of the individual must govern. The trainer should endeavor to keep the dog at a pitch wherein he delights to work every moment. If the dog potters betimes, or loafs, or is dilatory of execution, he loses accordingly if his opponent is industriously persistent and finished in his work.

The Derbys are considered by many as being puppy stakes, but they are so in name only. The age limit is necessarily so liberal that it permits the running of two-year-olds, a trifle more or less as to age, and at two years a dog may be considered as mature in relation to field work. The breeder should, there- fore, endeavor to have his puppies whelped as nearly on or after Jan. 1 is possible, thereby to obtain the greatest allowable age. Then they can be given quite a thorough training the fall and winter of their first season, beginning their second season as trained dogs prepared to take a post-graduate course, and to enlarge their practical experience.

In handling a dog in competition, the trainer should attend strictly to his own affairs. Any attempt to supervise or dictate to the opposing handler is impertinent and useless.

Any captiousness or insubordination in respect to the judges militates against the handler's success. If one handler obeys the "judges' instructions and the other does not, the judges will possibly after a while leave the disobedient handler to go where he pleases and do as he likes, the disobedience and refusal to follow the instructions justly being considered as inability to do so.

The judges will always give a respectful hearing to any complaints of interference made by a handler, if they are not frivolous or prejudiced in their ori- gin. However, it is much better to go through the competition looking out for the best interests of the dogs in charge rather than to engage in looking for trouble.

Some handlers school their dogs to disregard the whistle, or to go out the faster when they hear it, and this to guard against their being called in or turned at improper junctures by the whistling of the opposing handler.

There are but few handlers who do not whistle to and order their dogs too much when in competition. The less noise made, the better. Between heats the dog should be carried in a wagon. After a heat is ended he should have all the burrs, etc., picked out of his coat and from between his toes, and if the weather is at all cold or raw he should be blanketed and made comfortable.

CHAPTER XX

FIELD TRIAL JUDGING

THE field trial judge at the greatest trials is rarely other than thoroughly competent to fill the position. The many years of experience have given to him a thorough schooling in field trial principles and field trial management. Reporters, handlers and owners have also derived common field trial knowledge from greater experience, so that the field trials of the present are conducted on principles and rules in which all who are properly experienced readily concur.

The trials have fully demonstrated that field experience alone is an insufficient schooling for a field trial judge. There is now a sharply recognized distinction between following a dog for the purpose of killing birds over him, and following him to determine how his hunting qualities compare with those of some other dog or dogs, or what they are intrinsically in themselves. There is all the difference between the two instances that there is between a horse drawing a plow and a horse in a race; and yet the man who held a plow all his life very well might not be able to judge in a horse race very well. Indeed, there are many good shooters who can reap the best results from the work of a setter or pointer, yet who cannot explain in detail the essentials of good field work, nor wherein one manner of it is better or worse than another.

The field trial judge should have a perfect theoretical knowledge of the different degrees of the qualities which are recognized as being competitive, each as it concerns itself and as it relates to the others. This knowledge should be broadly supplemented with practical experience, so that he will be able to discern the real from the sham work displayed in actual competition, as, for instance, when two dogs are ranging alike in respect to speed and area of ground covered, yet one is running merely from high spirits, without using his nose industriously, while the other is working after the best manner, etc. Again, some dogs will hunt well with a dog which will take the initiative and lead them out. They like company and rivalry; they go as wide as their leader. Alone, such dogs might not take an independent cast of a hundred yards,

As nearly all field trial managements engage three judges, the third man may be a novice, although he should be an expert as to experience. This serves to graduate new material. With two competent experts the third man, whether he be competent or incompetent, will have no material effect on the results, for if he be competent he agrees with them, and if he be incompetent they outvote him and decide accordingly.

Contrary to the estimates of the inexperienced, the mere matter of deciding which is the better of two dogs, or the best of a lot of dogs, is but a small part of a judge's duties. He should have a good sense of location, so that after working out the grounds once or twice he will have a knowledge of their topographical features and the habitats of the birds. For each heat, when he knows their field trial resources, he can lay out a course which will equitably divide the grounds which contain birds and those which do not, with a due consideration of open and cover, so that there will be a free opportunity to display range and work in cover, the heat proceeding consecutively the while without any disorder.

The unskilled judge, in the matter of locality, is merely drifting about from place to place, running squarely against boundary lines which cannot be crossed, or creeks, or dense thickets, or farmyards, or places which are nowhere in particular, and no good at all, with the result that the dogs must be repeatedly called in, the whole party doubling back on itself and on its trail, imposing a general readjustment to make a new start, with a walk of a few hundred yards or a mile before new grounds can be reached.

The judge whose memory is bad as to locality is generally governed by his vision from point to point, so that, instead of a consecutive course planned out, the heat is a succession of disorganized readjustments, which either mar or destroy the competition. The dogs are hardly well started on one course before the handlers are directed to send them on another. The handlers become separated in searching for their respective dogs, or, one dog being well in hand when the new course is given, his handler hurries him ahead on it, while the other handler tarries far behind in an effort to turn or find his dog. When the heat ends, this kind of judge does not know where the wagons are which contain the dogs to be run in the next heat, and a wait is entailed before the next heat is begun.

Before a heat is begun the judges should carefully estimate where it will end, and direct the competitors to be at that place with their dogs in waiting. All such matters are now by expert judges managed with a precision which a few years ago would have been deemed impossible. Every detail is so provided for that it comes in its proper sequence.

A course when once laid out and the heat begun should be

followed with a reasonable degree of consistency. Any material deviation from it for a momentary advantage is sure to result in a serious disarrangement of the general plans.

There are many incidents which tend to change the course and disorganize the plans of inexperienced judges, not the least of which is the dramatic cry of

"Point, Judges !" made by a handler two or three hundred yards away from the announced course. The novice-judge, nine times out of ten, rides in a furious gallop to see the supposed point, and nearly as many times out of ten there is no point. It is an old, and many times successful, device on the part of the straggling handler, to draw the judges near him so that he will not have the trouble of walking back to the judges, nor disturb the range of his dog in turning and working him back on the true course.

Nor should the judges gallop out after the dogs which disappear for a few moments in ranging; for when the dogs so see the judges they will cast out further and further, working to the horses as they would do to their handlers, so that the judge who rides ahead of the handlers at all is seriously and directly interfering with the competition.

If the dog is trained properly for the competition, he will range to his handler; hence the spectacular galloping to the front is unnecessary aside from the display of brave horsemanship. If the dog will not range to his handler, it is a matter with which the judge has no concern as an assistant in the handling. Moreover, galloping about, right and left, here and there, is undignified and unnecessary. The handlers are entirely responsible for the handling of their dogs; the judges are responsible only for judging the dogs as the handlers display their merits.

When a dog is really lost, as a good dog will be at limes when on a point in a thicket, etc., it is a, matter of courtesy to assist in finding the lost dog in an ordinary manner. Half-broken or unmanageable dogs, however, should never induce the judges to leave their places behind the handlers.

The best judging distance is about twenty to thirty yards behind the handlers, when in the open fields. The judges can spread out from thirty to fifty yards, incidentally taking advantage of rises in the ground, to see the work of the dogs at a distance, and this without interfering with the range or the duties of the handlers. Their effort should be to see all the work done, without interfering in any way with the dog's opportunities.

If a handler cannot keep his dog on a course laid out for him by the judges, his delinquency in this respect is his own loss. It is unreasonable to expect the judges and all the rest of the field trial interests to follow the erratic course laid out by an unmanageable dog, although the new judge is not at all unlikely to attempt it ; less so than formerly, however.

A firm, good-tempered management of the handlers and a strict observance of fairness toward them will win their respect. The judges, however, should be supreme in dictating all that concerns the competition. No interference with their prerogative should be tolerated.

Any flurry on the part of the judges is certain to have a corresponding effect on the handlers and the competition. If the judges stampede at every cry of "Point F etc., there is sure to be what is termed in field trial parlance "hustling" on the part of the handlers. When the handlers note that the judges will not go in other than an orderly manner, they go in an orderly manner themselves.

A dog which will not hold his point or back till his handler can walk up to him has little claim to winning a field trial, even if he has competitive ability worthy of consideration at all. Steadiness is a matter of test quite as much as is any other quality, therefore there is no reason for unsteadiness on the part of the judges.

A matter of the first importance is to know when a heat is ended; that is to say, when the dogs in it have displayed fully such qualities as they have; and to know when all the dogs in a stake have shown the best competition of which they are capable. Generally speaking, all the competition in a stake, if handled by the judges so that the dogs will display their best qualities, tends to a certain definite climax, which brings certain dogs to the fore as the legitimate winners.

If the dogs* are overworked from heat to heat and thereby the natural climax of the competition is destroyed, there follows a series of anti-climax circum- stances which destroys all possibility of intelligent decisions. Some of the field trials of the past have not been free from such mistaken management on the part of the judges.

When all the dogs in a stake are run to a stand- still, they are all then on the same level as to performance and ability. An analogous case would be if the judges trotted till they were all so completely exhausted that they could not walk. If this procedure were kept up heat after heat, it is readily apparent that, from a racing standpoint, there would have been a long departure past the true racing climax.

When the true climax in a field trial is passed, the whole competitive situation begins to change. The judges may know which are the best dogs, but if they have run them to a standstill, dogs of inferior quality may apparently be making a better showing at the finish, Lucky finds, made by poor dogs, will still further aggravate the anti-climax, and a competition which was once well in hand and definite as to its results will then become indeterminate on the competition shown, and nothing is left for the judges but to settle it arbitrarily.

It is a most embarrassing situation for the judges when the best dogs have been run to a standstill, while others, less deserving, are fresher from unavoidable circumstance and accidental advantage, such as running in the cool parts of the day, or in better parts of the ground and with better opportunities on birds, and may make the best final showing.

The last impressions are the most realistic and the best remembered, so that the good work of the best dogs in the commencement of a trial is not so impressive as the good work of any kind of a dog at the conclusion, when the best dogs have been incapacitated from excessive competition.

There is always a small percentage of grumblers at field trials regardless of the wisdom of the management or the decisions of the judges, and of these the shallowest is generally the most assertive and the most malicious. The "kicker" is not obsolete at trials, though his numbers are not so great as they were formerly. Some men are constitutional kickers.

Whether at play or at business, their selfishness always dominates their will and blinds their judgment. Advertising their dogs, a love of notoriety, faulty information, etc., actuate others. But whatever the opinion of the multitude may be, the judge should not be influenced by it in the least. Just decisions as the judge himself evolves them should be the only consideration, regardless of who approves or disapproves. At best the opinion of the multitude is of little value. There will be sufficient diversity of opinion in it to prove almost anything.

Some men will have a better understanding of a dog's work in one day than some other men will have in a lifetime. The matter of brains and natural aptitude governs in this case as it does in all other branches of man's intelligent effort ; therefore it is essential that a field trial judge have that somewhat uncommon quality called common sense.

The! average man who has not by habit been schooled to concentration finds great difficulty in concentrating his thoughts on one subject for a prolonged period of time; indeed, without a prior schooling many men cannot do so, and some cannot do so longer than a few moments at a time. Men who are mentally indolent or incapable of concentration of mind are not of the material for good judges.

The field trial judge must keep his eye and mind on the

dog's work incessantly. Unless he sees the work done, he knows nothing about it. If he sees two dogs, one on point, the other on back, after they are established, he does not know but what the pointing dog may have stolen the point from the dog which is apparently backing. As for errors, if the judge's eye is off the dogs, they may be made and the negligent judge will never of his own knowledge know that they ever happened.

The good judge must constantly make mental comparison of the industry, range, bird sense, judgment, independence of action, accuracy, quickness, honest work to the gun, etc., free from crafty coaching by his handler and jealous rivalry of his competitor; therefore to master all the details of the competition he must have a good memory. All this, added to planning the course for each heat and directing the rendezvous for the wagons at the end of each heat, is quite sufficient to keep his mind occupied within and his attention engaged without. Thus it will be noted that a field trial is a much more ponderous affair to handle than are one or two dogs in actual field work.

In laying out a course for a heat, reference to giving the dogs a good consecutive run and reference to good courses for the other dogs should be considered.

Field trial clubs, as a rule, rent their grounds and within such territory they have all the needed rights and factors for giving the dogs the required competitive tests. The grounds vary greatly in character. In parts the birds are in generous abundance; in others there may be none at all. Some parts may be all cover, or mixed open and cover, or open entirely. Creeks, wire fences, swamps, steep hills, etc., are also circumstances which may require consideration. It is readily perceived that if the grounds are worked irregularly back and forth without any fixed plans or that if the choice parts are worked out first, then the dogs which run in the subsequent heats work on ground already more or less worked out, or they have to work on the poorest remaining ground. The judge, therefore, must approximately apportion his ground so that each brace will have a trial on un-worked ground, dividing the choice and poor parts as equitably as may be, so that the braces will have chances as near alike as intelligent planning can devise. If one dog finds and points a dozen bevies in a certain course, and another dog, working equally well in another course, finds no birds because there are none in it to find, the former would likely receive the approval of the green judge, who has yet to learn the value of opportunity or its absence. The trained judge has all such considerations in mind.

The next greatest affliction in comparison with the judge who is frantically intent on being everywhere at the same time, right or wrong, is the judge who has no ideas in respect to going anywhere. He is weak and indecisive, the competition lags and is weak in consequence, because he does not know where to go nor what to do.

Every few moments there is likely to be some matter submitted to him for a ruling, and, however good he may be in an actual day's shooting, if he is not competent as a judge he will be unable to conceal it. Indecision makes incompetency manifest, and the more incompetent he is the more rulings he will have to make, for error begets trouble and disorganization. Brave impartiality and energy when judging imaginary field trials in a circle of friends by the fire side, and the same when confronted by men who are sternly in earnest in a real trial, have quite different aspects.

The ready judgment of the irresponsible spectator who sees but little but whose conclusions are great is many times at the judge's service if he will but listen to him. It is a mistake to discuss the competition with any on-looker, as it is a mistake, directly or indirectly, in any way, to endeavor apologetically to explain any decision. If a contestant asks in good faith as to how his dog was beaten, it is quite proper to give him the needed information; however, the information being given, no argument concerning it should be permitted. In taking dogs into the second and subsequent series, the judge should be careful to estimate their performance on its class rather than on a mere matter of detail alone. A dog which shows good-class ability will repeat his good performance heat after heat, whereas the dog which made some accidental good work, or good work from advantageous circumstance, may be entirely incapable of repeating it. A man who cannot discriminate as to class will never make an accurate and sound judge of field trial competition. Where class work is considered, the competition works to a natural and definite conclusion; when it is ignored there may be the absurd spectacle of a low-class dog, competing for first at the final of a stake, with dogs of much higher ability left out of the competition. Nor should any dogs of inferior quality be taken into a series out of mere compliment to their owners. When a dog has shown himself inferior to other dogs, his part in the competition is determined and should be ended. To take an inferior dog into a series to which he is not entitled on his merits perpetrates a wrong on the other competitors, however much of a compliment it may be to the owner.

CHAPTER XXI

KENNEL MANAGEMENT

THE dog's sleeping quarters should be dry, clean, well ventilated and comfortable. He should have ample room in which to exercise, in default of which he should be given a good run night and morning each day. Exercise is indispensable to his physical and mental well-being.

Dogs should never be kept on chain. Old dogs in particular fret and worry, and in time become more or less soured in temper.

Young dogs, from standing in a set, strained position at the length of the chain, frequently grow up out of shape; their elbows turn out, their faces are wrinkled and bear an anxious expression, and they become addicted to habitual worry and irritation.

Cleanliness, good food, pure water, exercise and wholesome sleeping places are as necessary to the good health of the dog as they are to the good health of his master. Exercise, in fact, is more essential to the dog, for when he becomes fat his powers quickly degenerate. He then becomes indolent, deficient in stamina and predisposed to disease. With some dogs it is a matter of great difficulty to work off the fat, as they either will not or cannot work enough to reduce it other than by very slow degrees.

The food of the dog is worthy of much greater consideration than is commonly given to it. The table scraps of some families make quite good food, while those of other families cease to be food at all for any animal. There is quite a remove between scraps of good beef, bread, vegetables, etc., on the one hand, and potato skins on the other ; that is to say, table scraps, to be of food value, must have food constituents.

Sheeps' heads, tripe, mutton, beef, roasted rare or boiled with cabbage, turnips and onions, etc., make an excellent food. Corn-meal or any other purely vegetable food is unfit for the dog. He will live a shorter time, grow old younger and cease to be a working dog at an earlier age than he will on any other diet. The dog is carnivorous, and therefore he needs a meat diet. The ill effect of the latter, when such there is, is not from the meat diet of itself, but from over-feeding. In a state of nature the dog gets his meals at uncertain times, perhaps days apart. Once a day is quite often enough to feed him, yet the average dog owner is prone to judge of the dog's needs by his own, and therefore he feeds the dog three times a day with a few morsels, perhaps, between times.

The dog's digestive organs are not adapted to the assimilation of a vegetable diet. On this point, the following, taken from a paper read before the New England Kennel Club, Boston, July, 1884, by Dr. Billings, will be read with interest: "No matter in what way we look at it, the dog's ancestors were carnivorous, and the nature of their descendants has not changed in this regard, though, as in everything else, man has succeeded in changing it to a degree. Still, a carnivore he was, is and ever will be. He is not a masticator. He has not a grinding tooth in his head. He has nothing but biting and tearing teeth in the front, and crushers in the posterior part of the jaws. He takes no pleasure in eating as the chewers i. e. the masticating animals do. His is a feeling of emptiness, and when able he gulps his food, fills his stomach and, when he can do so, retires to a secluded spot to rest. It may be interpolated also that, in proportion to the size of the body, the canine family have the largest stomachs of any known species of animals.

"Critical persons need not think we have any reference to the receptive stomach of the ruminants; we mean the digestive stomach.

"The dog's natural food is meat, and to avoid giving them a strong odor we should cook it. Meal and starchy food is an abomination, and totally unfit for dogs, even the most delicate, though all the bigoted ignorance of all the dog men from time to eternity assert the contrary. The dog can live on the stuff, I admit, but it finds no organs for its preparation or digestion until it has passed through the stomach into the intestines. He has no grinders to prepare it in the mouth, and if he had he gulps it without chewing; his salivary glands are rudimentary, hence he has no means whatever of turning starchy food into sugar and dextrine, which fit them for nourishment, as ruminants have. Starchy food is not acted upon by the gastric juices to any great degree, and so they pass unchanged through the stomach into the beginning of the intestines, where the pancreas or salivary glands of the abdomen have to do all the work.

"Feeding on meat does not ruin the scent of sport- ing dogs as ignorance so frequently asserts. If it did, the whole wild canine race wolves, jackals, etc. would long ago have died of starvation. Feeding meat does not make dogs ugly, but confinement and neglect do. Finally, common sense and the study of the subject in all its details are better guides than the accumulated ignorance of the world on any subject."

The experience of all the eminent trainers and most advanced sportsmen fully bears out the foregoing. A dog will do more and better work on a meat diet than on any other, and he will also have better health and a longer life if so fed.

Many owners are prejudiced in favor of vegetable food as a matter of economy. There is no doubt of its relative cheapness, but that is quite another matter from its fitness,

Whether the dog is working or idling, one meal a day, at evening, is quite enough. The sympathy of the owner who judges his dog's needs by his own is wasted when he imagines that the dog will suffer from hunger if he has not three meals a day. Actual knowledge in this matter is much better than un- thinking sympathy.

Other Antiquarian titles you may enjoy from
Hand Thrown Books

ALL ABOUT TROUT FISHING
J. A. Riddell - 1909

"As an angler who has spent most of twenty five seasons by the riverside my aim is to convey to the reader, in simple language, the outcome of actual experience, in the hope that beginners, and also more experienced anglers, may find some information that will enlighten and assist them in attaining better piscatorial results."

AMERICAN PARTRIDGE AND
PHEASANT SHOOTING – 1877 – Frank Schley

Wherein the methods of hunting partridge, quail and ruffed grouse, tips on guns and dogs and the art of wing shooting are described. "Successful shooting is the ability to measure at a glance, 30 to 50 yards with certainty. Unless you learn to judge distances accurately when in the field, you will never become certain of stopping your birds."

CULTURE OF THE QUAIL
HOW TO RAISE QUAIL FOR PROFIT

Raising quail is a unique and interesting business, combining pleasure with few drawbacks. The quail is easily raised, cost very little to feed, are hardy, healthy and generally free from every contagious disease. The quail brings a better price than all other poultry providing for a decidedly profitable business having a good future before it.

DUCKING DAYS
1919 – An anthology

Narratives of duck hunting by famous outdoorsmen who had the good fortunate to have spent time on lakes, rivers and marshes during the Golden Age of hunting. "A Texas Duck Hunt" "Following the Redheads to the Gulf Coast" "On Missouri River Bars" "Duck Shooting on the Illinois River" more

DUCK SHOOTING AND HUNTING SKETCHES
1916 - William C. Hazelton

Narratives of Duck Hunting Experiences, Habits of Our Wild Fowl and Hunting Methods, Facts Concerning Migration, Breeding Grounds, Food and Articles about Some of Our Game Birds and Several Anecdotes on Hunting Dog Tales of the hunt from the Golden of Age of hunting on by-gone marshes, rivers and lakes.

FISHING AND SHOOTING SKETCHES
1909 – Grover Cleveland

This is a timeless collection of sporting tales by President Grover Cleveland who was both a dedicated hunter and fisherman; an experienced angler and excellent wing shooter. But he knew his shortcomings. On quail shooting, for instance he admitted. "I do not assume to be competent to give advice on shooting. I miss shots too often to undertake such a role."

FUR FEATHER & FIN – *Trout Series*
1904 – Alfred E. T. Watson

Anyone who is desirous of obtaining a fair share of piscatorial good fortune should take care that his fishing garb is sober of hue and not of a nature to attract the attention of the trout. Let your rod be light and gentle, and let not your line exceed three or four hairs at the most; but if you can attain to angle with one hair, you shall have more rises and catch more fish. *Trout Wisdom*

FUR FEATHER & FIN – *Snipe & Woodcock Series*
1903 – Alfred E. T. Watson

For the sportsman memories of upland hunts for either bird evokes arguments favoring one over the other. Such is the depth of feelings experienced when seeking sport with these little game birds. Fur Feather and Fin **Snipe & Woodcock Series** first published in 1903 explores the habits, haunts and shooting techniques of these elusive denizens of the uplands.

GAME FARMING
1915 – A Hercules Powder Company Publication

Game Farming provides step by step instructions on the breeding and preservation of quail, partridge, pheasant, wild duck and grouse. Contained in this extensive reference book is information to their natural feed, habitat, the control of natural enemies. It focuses on the need, based on the excesses of unchecked hunting practices for restoration of game through the application of responsible breeding practices.

JIST HUNTING
1921 – Ozark Ripley

"Ozark Ripley loves the outdoors, the far horizons and dogs. And every dog I have ever known loved Ozark. A man who loves dogs and is loved by dogs always rings true." Ozark shares his experiences with rod, gun and old mother earth immersed in the outdoors with only frying pan, a bag of flour, a bit of bacon, a blanket, rushing, streams, wind kissed waters, and woodland trails.

LAKE FIELD AND FORREST
1899 – Frank A. Bates

A wonderful collection of stories by self proclaimed "sportsman-naturalist" Frank Bates. Published in 1899 his stories paint a lavish picture of a golden era of hunting and fishing that thankfully has been preserved through the journals and writings of sportsmen like Bates of that time.

PHEASANT FARMING
A DETAILED "HOW TO"

IN AMERICA we have been very wasteful of our natural our resources. This is especially the case in the destruction of our game birds. That we must produce, if we would destroy has finally dawned on us. Propagation is the only solution of the future game supply problem.

PRACTICAL DRY FLY FISHING
1912 - Emlyn M. Gill

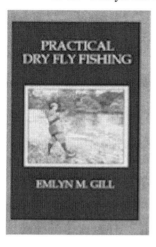

The subject has been fully covered by a number of expert writers who have lived in the home of the dry-fly, England.

With the exception of a few magazine articles, there has been little American Literature upon the subject. This work is confined to the floating fly. The beauties of nature, one of the chief attractions of a day on the trout stream, are left to the poetic pens of English literature.

SCATTERGUN SKETCHES
1922 – Horatio Bigelow

WHEN business binds and you can't seem to get away on that long anticipated shooting trip, you can find relief in the "Call of the Wild". When gathered around the camp-fire how often have you heard the "old timers" spin the yarns that linger with you? These are those yarns from long ago told with wit and an eye for detail which will carry you back.

SPECKLED BROOK TROUT
1902 – Various authors

The brook trout has long held a special place in the hearts and minds of anglers. Lavishly illustrated this volume, a collection from the pens of a number of well known writers, begins by supplying general information on the wily brookie, before moving on to discuss habitat, habits and angling methods then finally culinary considerations.

TALES OF DUCK AND GOOSE SHOOTING
1922 – William C. Hazelton

Whether hunted for food or to show skill with a gun some imperative causes man reject all creature comforts, brave exposure to nasty weather, or risk the danger of accidental mutilation or death. Along with the duck season comes a longing to fondle a gun and sit staring at the ammunition box. This wonderful collection recounts stories from the golden era of water fowling.

THE ART OF WING SHOOTING
1895 – William Bruce Leffingwell

The Art of Wing Shooting is a practical treatise on the use of the shot gun. Illustrated by sketches and easy to read it guides you to become an expert shot. It contains a complete expose of the scientific use of the shot gun along with an examination of the habits and resorts of game birds and waterfowl. And how to become a proficient inanimate target shot.

THE BOYS BOOK OF HUNTING AND FISHING
1914 – Warren H. Miller

"There is but one excuse for the men of to-day and that is to prepare boys by instilling in them an enduring appreciation for the great outdoors; undoubtedly a good thing." This work is devoted to the proper use of rod and gun to provide an opportunity to go to the open for their games and recreation with the helping hand of an exhaustive book on sports of the outdoor world.

THE IDYL OF THE SPLIT BAMBOO
1920 – George Parker Holden

The fisherman's transcendent implement is his rod. While few anglers might undertake making a split cane rod it requires little to convince anyone that fishermen love to tinker with their tackle. If you can make a rod you certainly can fix one. Building a split-bamboo rod is an operation in overcoming those particular difficulties in handling and working bamboo which give the most trouble

THE SPORTING DOG
1904 – Joseph A. Graham

It's commonly conceded that Great Britain provided the stock all our dogs of sporting breed. So how do they differ from the British dogs? Reduced to the simplest terms they are faster, lighter and quicker in action." *The Sporting Dog*" is a fascinating study of the development of the American hunting dog.

TRAINING THE HUNTING DOG
1901 – B. Waters

Dog training, considered as an art, has no mysteries, no insurmountable obstacles, and unfortunately no short cuts. It is a result of patient schooling analogous to that employed in the training a child. In this case however the trainees are being prepared for limited service in the pursuit of game. Full of practical, usable, effective training methods it is as relevant today as it was 100 years ago.

TROUT FISHING FOR BEGINNERS
Richard Clapham

The perfect gift for either the beginning trout angler or the seasoned angler who can occasionally use a gentle reminder of how often ignoring the basics of the sport can lead to an empty creel. This is a wonderful little classic that should be a part of every sportsman's library.

TROUT FISHING IN AMERICA
1914 – Charles Zibeon Southard

The author attempts to settle once and for all the raging controversy over whether it is better to embrace the dry fly or wet fly school of fly fishing. And while this topic remains unresolved this classic is a richly warm and extensively useful volume on virtually every aspect of fly fishing for trout. From rod to reel, from line to leader no stone in the stream is left unturned.

THE WILDERNESS HOME
1908 – Oliver Kemp

IF you love the out-of-doors, this book was written for you, to crystallize and bring into reality that vague longing which you have felt for a lodge in the wilderness.

Somewhere the trail has led you to the ideal spot in the deep forest, by the shores of a smiling lake or within sound of the murmuring waters.

WING SHOOTING
1881 – Anonymous

The author in "Wing Shooting" provides full directions for the various methods of loading the modern breach-loader, along with instructions concerning powder, shot and wadding. Also covered are general hints on wing shooting together with instructive and positive methods for hunting snipe, woodcock, grouse and quail.

WOODCOCK SHOOTING
1908 – Edmund Davis

Lazy days spent in the uplands inevitably bring a closer connection with nature; especially when your sport is seeking that wily little game bird, the woodcock. For the woodcock reassures us that the brooks are still dancing merrily through the woods and are on their way to sweet scented meadows. So it is, the woodcock brings joy to the lovers of forest, cover and stream.

IF HE'S DEAD NOW HE'LL BE DEAD IN THE MORNING
2012 – J. C. Dougherty

Tales of full creels, full waders and the all too occasional perfect point from a snazzy setter. Revisit with the author crisp autumn days wandering bird-less through the woods, or sunny spring afternoons casting about for un-cooperative trout. These are stories of life-long friends and life-long laughs. Journal of a Somewhat Amusing Outdoor Life is the perfect gift for the sportsman in your life.

AN EDIBLE MEMOIR   2014 -   J. C. Dougherty

Where north meets south; from grits to game birds Recipes and tall tales about the big ones that got away and the collard greens that couldn't. Black Eye Pea Fritters with Onion Jam ~ Woodcock Pie ~ Cajun Fried Bullfrog ~ Hush Puppies ~ Fried Grits ~ Duck Soup with White Beans ~ Fried Catfish Southern Fried Chicken ~ Okra Fried to within an inch of its life!

THE ART OF RESTORING SPLIT CANE FLY RODS.
2012 – J. C. Dougherty

Split cane bamboo fly rods are not for everyone, some people are too addicted to high tech. Bamboo rods only warm the heart and are in tune with the rhythms of the rivers streams and lakes they touch. And there's little else that is as satisfying as bringing one of these classic rods back to life. Advice, tips and instructions on how to repair cracks, splits broken ferrules cork grip and more.

Hand Thrown Books

West Newbury, MA
www.handthrownbooks.com

Printed in Great Britain
by Amazon

85085969R00127